GU00986192

Vafþrúðnismál
Second edition

Edited with an introduction and notes by
TIM WILLIAM MACHAN

Probably composed at the height of the Viking Age, *Vafþrúðnismál* recounts how one day the mysterious and powerful god Óðinn visits the hall of an ancient giant named Vafþrúðnir. There, with their heads wagered over the outcome, the two engage in a wisdom contest about how the world was created, who inhabits it, and what will come of it when the gods and giants battle one last time at the world-ending Ragnarǫk. The qualities that popular imagination sees in the Vikings – bravery, courage, and cunning – are the very qualities that the two adversaries display in their deadly game. By the time the game ends, and the poem with it, the reader has witnessed a vista not only of the terror and mystery of medieval Scandinavia but of its beauty as well.

Durham University
Centre for Medieval
and Renaissance Studies

Durham Publications in Medieval and Renaissance Studies
General Editor Dr Giles E.M. Gasper

Durham Medieval and Renaissance Texts
Series Editor Professor John McKinnell

Durham Medieval and Renaissance Monographs and Essays
Series Editors Professor David Cowling and Professor David Rollason

DURHAM MEDIEVAL AND RENAISSANCE TEXTS 1

Vafþrúðnismál

Second edition

Edited with an introduction and notes by

TIM WILLIAM MACHAN

Centre for Medieval and Renaissance Studies, Durham University

Pontifical Institute of Mediaeval Studies, Toronto

Library and Archives Canada Cataloguing in Publication

Vafþrúðnismál / edited by Tim William Machan. – 2nd ed.

(Durham medieval and renaissance texts, 1758–0331 ; 1)
Introduction in English, text in Old Norse.
Co-published by the Centre for Medieval and Renaissance Studies,
    Durham University.
Includes bibliographical references and index.
ISBN 978–0–88844–561–2

    1. Eddas.   2. Mythology, Norse.   3. Eddas – History and criticism.
4. Old Norse poetry – History and criticism.   I. Machan, Tim William
II. University of Durham. Centre for Medieval and Renaissance Studies
III. Series.

PT7237.V33 2008   839'.61   C2008–904841–5

Pontifical Institute of Mediaeval Studies
59 Queen's Park Crescent East
Toronto, Ontario, Canada M5S 2C4
www.pims.ca

MANUFACTURED IN CANADA

CONTENTS

ABBREVIATIONS

Manuscripts

A   Reykjavík, Stofnun Árna Magnússonar, MS AM 748 I 4to

R   Reykjavík, Stofnun Árna Magnússonar, MS GkS 2365 4to

R^2 Reykjavík, Stofnun Árna Magnússonar, MS GkS 2367 4to

T   Utrecht, University Library, MS 1374

U   Uppsala, University Library, MS DG 11

W   Copenhagen, Arnamagnæan Institute, MS AM 242 fol

Eddic Poems

Akv.   *Atlaqviða in grœnlenzca*

Alv.   *Alvíssmál*

Am.   *Atlamál in grœnlenzco*

Bdr.   *Baldrs draumar*

Fm.   *Fáfnismál*

Grm.   *Grímnismál*

Hv.   *Hávamál*

HHI   *Helgaqviða Hundingsbana in fyrri*

HHII   *Helgaqviða Hundingsbana ǫnnor*

Hrbl.   *Hárbarðzlióð*

Hym.   *Hymisqviða*

Ls.   *Locasenna*

Rm.   *Reginsmál*

Rþ.   *Rígsþula*

Sd.   *Sigrdrífomál*

Skm.   *For Scírnis*

Vaf.   *Vafþrúðnismál*

Vkv.   *Vǫlundarqviða*

Vsp.   *Vǫluspá*

Þrk.   *Þrymsqviða*

ACKNOWLEDGMENTS

This edition, like all editions published by Durham Medieval Texts, is intended for beginning students. While it is hoped that advanced scholars will find a separate edition of *Vafþrúðnismál* useful, the presumed audience of this book is the student who is only generally acquainted with Old Norse language and literature and who is reading Eddic poetry for the first time. The Introduction, accordingly, discusses the various codicological, philological and cultural factors which determine Eddic poetry and which are requisite for any understanding of it. *Vafþrúðnismál* seems a particularly good text to serve as an introduction to the *Poetic Edda*, for its repetitions, dialogue format, and familiar legends make it more accessible than other poems.

In preparing this edition I have drawn on the help and goodwill of several people, whose contributions I am grateful to have the opportunity to recognize. I would like to thank Richard N. Ringler, with whom I first studied Old Norse language and literature, and John C. McGalliard, who encouraged my interest. John S. McKinnell has been a scrupulous editor, and this edition has benefited in many important ways from his knowledge of Eddic poetry. Richard N. Ringler and R.I. Page also read and improved earlier versions of this book. Christine Marie Machan shared her expertise on the modern Scandinavian languages and offered invaluable encouragement and support throughout this undertaking. Finally, I would like to thank the staff of Memorial Library of Marquette University, for efficiently acquiring a number of obscure but essential materials, and the Marquette University Committee on Research, for granting me a Summer Faculty Fellowship which enabled me to complete this book.

TWM
Wauwatosa, 1988

PREFACE TO THE SECOND EDITION

Revising a book twenty years after it first appeared is challenging: one wants to change everything or nothing. Inevitably, I've tried to take a middle ground, updating and correcting as appropriate but leaving enough of the original to maintain the qualities that I hope made the book useful in the first place. To this end, I've revised all parts of the discussion in light of recent scholarship, edited portions in light of reviewers' comments, and worked to make the style continually accessible to beginning students, who remain this book's primary audience. While the Durham Series volumes have expanded in audience and scope, my over-riding goal has likewise remained the same – to provide an introduction to Eddic poetry, in its original language and with all its textual and interpretive complexities and uncertainties, for readers who are just beginning the study of Old Norse.

I'm grateful to Paul Bibire and Fred Unwalla for all their technical help with the volume, and to John McKinnell who first saw its merit, suggested the utility of a revised edition, and provided a wealth of valuable commentary and suggestions for this revision. Without doubt, the book is much better – not to mention simply possible – because of all their efforts.

TWM
2008

Gods and heroes, giants and monsters – the supernatural has always captured the human imagination. We tell stories to explain and understand such phenomena, and in the process, we hope, gain control of the often terrifying and sometimes overpowering world in which we live. These stories help us to understand our place in the universe, to remember our past and to imagine a future, to hold tight to hope and a belief that a better world is possible. If they are good enough stories, they may even allow us to see ourselves in the heroes and thereby hold our own monsters at bay. *Vafþrúðnismál* tells such a story.

Probably composed at the height of the Viking Age, the poem recounts how one day the mysterious and powerful god Óðinn visits the hall of an ancient giant named Vafþrúðnir. There, with their heads wagered over the outcome, the two engage in a wisdom contest about how the world was created, who inhabits it, and what will come of it when the gods and giants battle one last time at the world-ending Ragnarǫk. The qualities that popular imagination sees in the Vikings – bravery, courage, and cunning – are the very qualities that the two adversaries display in their deadly game. By the time the game ends, and the poem with it, the reader has witnessed a vista not only of the terror and mystery of medieval Scandinavia but of its beauty as well.

Like most Norse artifacts, whether helmets or poems, *Vafþrúðnismál* has survived to the present by the slenderest means. For the Vikings, poetry was neither solitary nor permanent but communal and ephemeral. It was meant for oral presentation in a hall much like Vafþrúðnir's, and this means that individuals were primarily exposed to poetry in group settings, where the audience's response, irretrievably lost to us, could be as much a part of the poetic experience as the poem's words and the poet's delivery. It also means that the poems survive not in hundreds and thousands of copies, as is the case with modern fiction, but in isolated, often damaged manuscripts. But although our knowledge of the medieval world rests on slender evidence, witnesses like *Vafþrúðnismál* still have much to say about the Viking world.

Manuscripts, Date, and Provenance

Vafþrúðnismál survives in its entirety apparently only in Reykjavík, Stofnun Árna Magnússonar, MS GkS 2365 4to (R), the famous Codex Regius, where it is the third poem. Approximately the last two-thirds of the text preserved in R are also extant in Reykjavík, Stofnun Árna Magnússonar, MS AM 748 I 4to (A). Nine stanzas or partial stanzas are quoted by Snorri Sturluson in *Gylfaginning*, the first part of the *Prose Edda*. The four manuscripts with independent textual authority of Snorri's *Edda* are: Reykjavík, Stofnun Árna Magnússonar, MS GkS 2367 4to (R^2), Utrecht, University Library, MS 1374 (T), Uppsala, University Library, MS DG 11 (U), and Copenhagen, Arnamagnæan Institute, MS AM 242 fol (W).

R is perhaps the most famous of all the Old Norse manuscripts, but despite centuries of study, its date, provenance, and purpose remain controversial. Even the significance of the traditional name by which the collective poems of R are known – the *Poetic Edda* – has raised controversy.[1] Given the scope of this edition, consequently, the following discussion of R in particular and the *Poetic Edda* in general attempts only to delineate the controversies, not to resolve them.

Dating from about 1270 and written in Iceland,[2] R contains twenty-nine mythic and heroic poems and a number of prose links between and within the poems. The first eleven poems concern the

---

1   Anthony Faulkes, "Edda," *Gripla* 2 (1977): 32–39.

2   Andreas Heusler, ed., *Codex Regius of The Elder Edda* (Copenhagen, 1937), 16.

tales and sayings of the gods, while the remaining ones relate the stories of Sigurðr and the Vǫlsungar. Though one scribe copied the entirety of R, a number of palaeographic, orthographic, and phonological differences among individual texts indicates that at the very least the mythic and heroic poems were copied from different written sources, and smaller collections, such as one involving *Vǫluspá, Vafþrúðnismál,* and *Grímnismál,* may have existed as well.[3] The latter two in particular, which are so ordered in both R and A, share several verbal, thematic, and codicological connections. The arrangement of the poems in R would not seem to be fortuitous, and various attempts have been made to isolate the rationale of the compiler. Klingenberg, for instance, contends that *Helgaqviða Hundingsbana in fyrri,* the first of the heroic poems, was intentionally written and joined to the mythic poems to imply the fulfilment of the tragedies adumbrated in *Vǫluspá* and that the subsequent heroic poems further develop this theme. This argument has some codicological and thematic difficulties, but as Harris has observed, "Klingenberg's recognition that an 'idea' informs the book [i.e. R] as a whole and, to some extent, his characterization of that 'idea' constitute an exciting step forward in the codicology of the Codex Regius."[4]

---

3   Gustaf Lindblad, *Studier i Codex Regius av äldre Eddan* (Lund, 1954) and "Poetiska Eddans förhistoria och skrivskicket i Codex regius," *Arkiv för nordisk filologi* 95 (1980): 142–67, at 160; Heusler, *Codex Regius of The Elder Edda,* 25; Terry Gunnell, *The Origins of Drama in Scandinavia* (Woodbridge, UK; Rochester, NY, 1995), 203–6.

4   Heinz Klingenberg, *Edda: Sammlung und Dichtung* (Basel, 1974); Joseph Harris, "Eddic Poetry," in *Old Norse-Icelandic Literature: A Critical Guide,* ed. Carol J. Clover and John Lindow (Ithaca, 1985), 68–156, at 78. For more details of the date, history, and physical appearance of R, see Heusler, *Codex Regius of The Elder Edda,* and Ursula Dronke, ed., *The Poetic Edda,* vol. 1: *The Heroic Poems* (Oxford, 1969), xi–xiii.

Consideration of R in conjunction with A and the manuscripts of the *Prose Edda* provides only minor clarification for the date and origin of the manuscript. Probably originating at the end of the thirteenth century,[5] A contains only *Vafþrúðnismál, Grímnismál, For Scírnis, Hárbarðzlióð, Hymisqviða,* the beginning of *Volundarqviða,* and *Baldrs draumar,* which does not occur in R. Moreover, the ordering of the poems in A lacks the logic of that in R. The differences between the manuscripts may thus imply, *a priori,* that A is a selective and ineffective rearrangement of the text preserved in R, or that R is a refinement of the text preserved in A. There is little doubt, however, that the texts of individual poems in R and A derive from a common written source. As Wessén observes, such derivation "appears with certainty from the almost verbal agreement in the wording of the text. Of special evidential force in this respect are the prose pieces. Further, it appears from the common errors and fortuitous coincidences of spelling."[6] For *Vafþrúðnismál* in particular, the general verbal similarity between the manuscripts suggests a common source, as do the textual problems in stanzas 27, 31, and 40. Similarities in abbreviations at 22.1–3 and even in the contractions and inflectional abbreviations for scattered individual words point to this same conclusion.[7] The manuscripts of Snorri's *Edda* are all later than R and A: R^2 dates from about 1325; T, a paper text, from about 1595, though it is believed to be a copy of an earlier manuscript; U from the early fourteenth century; and W from the mid-fourteenth century.[8]

5   Elias Wessén, ed., *Fragments of The Elder and The Younger Edda* (Copenhagen, 1945), 16.

6   Wessén, *Fragments of The Elder and The Younger Edda,* 21.

7   R.C. Boer, ed., *Die Edda mit historisch-kritischem Commentar* (Haarlem, 1922), 1: xii and 2: 51.

8   Elias Wessén, ed., *Codex Regius to The Younger Edda,* by Snorri Sturluson (Copenhagen, 1940), 6; Anthony Faulkes, ed., *Codex Trajectinus: The Utrecht Manuscript of the Prose Edda* (Copenhagen, 1985), 16; Anders Grape, ed., *Snorre Sturlasons Edda, Uppsala Håndskriften DG 11* (Stockholm, 1962–77), 2: ix; Sig-

Since in *Gylfaginning* (composed around 1220) Snorri draws heavily upon *Vǫluspá*, *Vafþrúðnismál*, and *Grímnismál*, and since all of the *Prose Edda* may be said to be infused with the spirit of the *Poetic Edda*, it has long been believed that Snorri himself could have played some part in the compilation of the source of R. Heusler and Wessén, for instance, contend that it was perhaps Snorri who caused some of the poems to be recorded initially and that at the very least it was Snorri's example that led others to search out and write down other poems in what Harris has described as "field trips in the manner of the nineteenth-century folklore collectors."[9] Other scholars suggest that Snorri was not responsible for recording any of the poems but only that, in the words of Sigurður Nordal, "the impulse to collect and write down the Eddaic lays proceeded from the Edda. Snorri himself does not seem to have had any written collection of them, at any rate one similar to that preserved in Codex Regius."[10] Complicating any arguments about the lays' origin is the fact that at least some of the Eddic poems seem to have existed in written form before the composition of the Codex Regius. Small gatherings of poems may have circulated, and Jón Steffensen has argued that whoever compiled the *Poetic Edda* was working in part from carved rune-staves.[11] *Vafþrúðnismál* is one of the poems that apparently existed in a manuscript before Snorri, since the use of ð for

urður Nordal, ed., *Codex Wormianus (The Younger Edda)*, by Snorri Sturluson (Copenhagen, 1931), 5.

9 Heusler, *Codex Regius of The Elder Edda*, 31–32; Wessén, *Fragments of The Elder and The Younger Edda*, 20; Harris, "Eddic Poetry," 76.

10 Nordal, *Codex Wormianus*, 12.

11 Steffensen, "Hugleiðingar um Eddukvæði," *Árbók hins íslenzka fornleifafélags* (1968): 26–38, at 36. Since Icelandic runic inscriptions seem not to appear until the thirteenth century, such a theory would require a Norwegian origin for at least some of the poems. See Anders Bæksted, *Islands Runeindskrifter* (Copenhagen, 1942).

the voiceless fricative (see below) would seem to imply a date of about 1200 for the earliest written version of the poem. According to Lindblad, a small, early collection consisting only of *Vafþrúðnismál* and *Grímnismál* was expanded under Snorri's direction to a greater mythic gathering. This original gathering was unmethodical and is preserved in A, and it was the redactor of R who first ordered the mythic gathering and combined it with the heroic one, which also existed inchoately before Snorri.[12]

While the date of R has been more or less established as about 1270, the date of its written archetype is less clear, as are the date and provenance of the earliest versions of individual poems. Lindblad has argued that the written source of most of the poems in R dates to about 1200–1240,[13] with *Vafþrúðnismál*, as I noted above, falling at the earlier end of this range. The date of the ultimate, oral origin of a given poem depends, of course, upon the poem in question, and Eddic poems have been variously dated from about 850 to a period contemporaneous with R. For linguistic and literary reasons, the initial composition of *Vafþrúðnismál* is generally set in the tenth century.[14] The forms *Reiðgotom* (12.5) and *reca* (53.3) reflect preliterate forms, and the use of the particle *um* in a variety of preverbal contexts similarly implies an early date (see notes to 11.3, 12.5, and 53.3). Additional linguistic evidence of an early date is the fact that the strong masculine accusative singular of the adjective *hverr* is regularly *hverian*, rather than *hvern*, for the di-

---

12 See the following studies by Lindblad: *Studier i Codex Regius*, 270; "Centrala eddaproblem i 1970-talets forsknings läge," *Scripta Islandica* 28 (1977): 3–26, at 18–21; "Snorre Sturlasson och eddadiktningen," *Saga och sed* (1978): 17–34, at 30–32; "Poetiska Eddans förhistoria," 160–61.

13 Lindblad, *Studier i Codex Regius*, 273.

14 So Finnur Jónsson, *Den oldnorske og oldislandske litteraturs historie*, vol. 1 (Copenhagen, 1920), 143, and Barbro Söderberg, "Formelgods och Eddakronologi," *Arkiv för nordisk filologi* 101 (1986), 50–86.

syllabic form is found predominately in texts considered old.[15] Though they might simply be poetically licensed archaisms, the *hverian* forms occur with a regularity that suggests that they are authentic: in six of the seven occurrences this disyllabic form is metrically necessary, while in 43.4 it is at least as likely as the monosyllabic form. Several critics use the poet's intimate knowledge of the mythological world as a dating criterion, stylistically grouping *Vafþrúðnismál* with *Grímnismál*, *Vǫluspá*, *Alvíssmál* and perhaps *Locasenna* as a poem imbued with heathen sensibility and therefore likely to be an early composition. Boer, for instance, regards the eschatological concerns of *Vafþrúðnismál* and *Vǫluspá* as a response to the introduction of Christianity in Scandinavia and so dates both poems to the tenth century.[16]

Of course, a thorough knowledge of mythology need not require an origin in pagan days. It might be argued that few medieval Scandinavians knew as much about Norse mythology as Snorri Sturluson, and he lived in a thoroughly Christian era. Similarly, the fact that *Vafþrúðnismál* and *Grímnismál* display familiarity with heathen matters and even at times seem to speak reverently about the gods (e.g. phrases like *in sváso goð* at 17.6) need not imply a tenth-century origin, for a traditional phrase

15   Adolf Noreen, *Altnordische Grammatik*, vol. 1: *Altisländische und altnorwegische Grammatik (Laut- und Flexionislehre) unter Berücksichtigung des Urnordischen*, 4th ed. (1923; rpt. Tubingen, 1970), §474.3. Bjarne Fidjestøl has argued that the statistical frequency of *of / um* is in fact one of the few reliable dating criteria, with higher frequency generally indicating an earlier date. With the third highest frequency in the *Poetic Edda*, *Vafþrúðnismál* would date to the tenth or even ninth century in his analysis. See *The Dating of Eddic Poetry: A Historical Survey and Methodological Investigation*, ed. Odd Einar Haugen (Copenhagen, 1999), 207–30.

16   Boer, *Die Edda*, 2: 59. See further B. Sijmons, ed., *Die Lieder der Edda: Text* (Halle, 1906), cccxliii; Jón Helgason, "Norges og Islands Digtning," in *Litteratur-historie B: Norge og Island*, ed. Sigurður Nordal (Stockholm, 1953), 96; and Jan de Vries, *Altnordische Literaturgeschichte*, 2nd ed., (Berlin, 1964–67), 1: 44–45.

might still be used in formulaic poetry after it had lost its original significance.[17] And in a different vein, despite his occasionally blatant irony, Snorri still thought highly enough of the gods as literary matter to devote considerable effort to recording their adventures. Anything like a heathen sensibility may thus be only antiquarianism or the inheritance of an earlier poetic tradition.

From an archeological perspective, Turville-Petre has suggested that the reference to Scinfaxi in stanza 12 mirrors the early Bronze Age Trundholm disc, which he believes may represent the sun being drawn across the sky by a chariot.[18] If the disc does represent the sun and if Scinfaxi does evoke the same concept, then the poem, too, could be early. But even this evidence is not unequivocal, for bits of early stories can survive undigested in later redactions; when Malory describes Gawain's strength as gradually increasing until midday and subsequently declining, he preserves a trait from some vegetation myth that has nothing to do with Camelot. Moreover, *Vafþrúðnismál* is perhaps not so thoroughly heathen as was once thought, for it contains at least one passage which seems to show the influence of Christianity: the *morgindǫggvar* of 45.4 apparently echo the manna of Exodus (see note).

All of this is not to deny an early date for *Vafþrúðnismál*. The tenth century still seems the most likely. But on the basis of the available evidence this date is perhaps the most likely for linguistic, not literary, reasons. The latter sometimes seem to be only extensions of a discredited nineteenth-century desire to identify, and perhaps eliminate, the Christian "coloring" in Germanic literature.

---

17   Cf. Lindblad, "Centrala eddaproblem," 9.

18   Gabriel Turville-Petre, *Myth and Religion of the North*: *The Religion of Ancient Scandinavia* (London, 1964), 5, and "Fertility of Beast and Soil in Old Norse Literature," in *Old Norse Literature and Mythology*: *A Symposium*, ed. Edgar C. Polomé (Austin, 1969), 244–64, at 245–47.

If *Vafþrúðnismál* and other Eddic poems did originate in the tenth century, they were presumably originally oral compositions (see below), and the poem would thus have been transmitted orally until the early thirteenth century. But the provenance of the earliest, oral Eddic poems – and, later, that of the earliest written ones – is as problematic as many other aspects of Eddic study. Were the poems composed in Iceland or Norway? Since R was certainly written in Iceland, most scholars had perhaps tacitly agreed that it was the place where the poems were composed until a series of articles by Didrik Seip contended that R was in fact a copy of a Norwegian manuscript.[19] And other critics have identified two additional bits of evidence that may imply a Norwegian original for *Vafþrúðnismál* in particular. First, the apparently erroneous reading *fróðan* for *svinnan* at 34.2 (see note) may derive from confusion between *f* and an initial long *s*, and this would be the case only if the archetype of R and A had used the long *s* found on the Continent.[20] And second, *holt* at 45.3 seems to refer to a grove or forest, and while such forests existed in Norway, any trees native to Iceland were small and scattered.[21]

Yet the case for continental composition is scarcely irrefutable. The *holt* of 45.3, for example, might express the apparently later Icelandic sense, "rocky outcrop." And Seip's detailed arguments have their own difficulties. Kuhn, for example, assembled an abundance of orthographic and paleographic evidence to argue that the features Seip had

19 Seip, "Har nordmenn skrevet opp Edda-diktningen?" *Maal og Minne* (1951): 3–33, "On the Original of the Codex regius of the Elder Edda," in *Studies in Honor of Albert Morey Sturtevant* (Lawrence, KY, 1952), 103–6, and "Om et norsk skriftlig grunnlag for Edda-diktningen eller deler av den," *Maal og Minne* (1957): 81–195. Also see note 11 above.

20 In addition to Seip's articles, see Evert Salberger, "Ett stavrimsproblem i Vafþrúðnismál 34," *Maal og Minne* (1955): 113–20, at 120.

21 Bertil Ejder, "Eddadikten Vafþrúðnismál," *Årsbok: Vetenskaps Societeten i Lund* (1960): 5–20, at 19.

identified as indicative of a Norwegian original were in fact common to all Icelandic manuscripts of the twelfth and thirteen centuries for the simple reason that Icelandic scribal practices derived from Norwegian ones. Kuhn also suggested that the language of R was only a literary dialect and thus provided few absolute clues to its geographic origins. Following up on Kuhn's work, indeed, Stefán Karlsson subsequently questioned the possibility of tracing any Icelandic manuscripts to Norwegian originals.[22]

And so the issue of origins is far from resolved, with the situation not at all as clear as Seip, on the one side, and Kuhn, on the other, suggested. Lindblad has noted, for instance, that the language of R has far more heterogeneity than Kuhn implies.[23] But however and wherever it originally came into existence, *Vafþrúðnismál* apparently experienced relatively little alteration in its transmission, perhaps because, as Finnur Jónsson observes, the dialogue form in conjunction with the contents of the poem left little opportunity for innovation.[24] The archetype of all authorities was probably at least one copy removed from the first written copy of the poem, for the readings at stanzas 27 and 40 (see notes) in all authorities imply a common, defective reading. Variation between R and A, including *of* in the latter wherever the former has *um*, is minimal and presumably due for the most part to scribal idiolect or unintentional scribal alteration. In fact, there are only four substantively significant differences between the texts that are not easily explicable as mechanical copying errors, and even these are fairly trans-

22 Hans Kuhn, "Die norwegischen Spuren in der Liederedda," *Acta Philologica Scandinavica* 22 (1954): 65–80, at 79, and "Zur Grammatik und Textgestaltung der älteren Edda," *Zeitschrift für deutsches Altertum* 90 (1960–61): 241–68, at 261; Stefán Karlsson, "Om norvagismer i islandske håndskrifter," *Maal og Minne* (1978): 87–101.

23 Lindblad, "Centrala eddaproblem," 23.

24 Finnur Jónsson, *Den oldnorske*, 114.

parent; that at 30.2 probably derives from anticipation by the scribe of A of the same formula as in 26.2 and 28.2; that at 36.6 suggests an attempt by the scribe of A to clarify a rather awkward construction; that at 40–41 very likely involves a reconstruction by the scribe of R (see note); and that at 51.6 is probably due to confusion by the scribe of R. An edition of A (as much of it as exists) would require more grammatical emendation than one of R, but the text of A is still in the main quite good.

Differences between R and A, on the one hand, and R^2, T, U, and W, on the other, are more numerous, though again they are of a fairly trivial sort (e.g. 31.3 and 35.2). The more substantive variants in U (e.g. 31.3, 31.4, 35.5, and 45.4–6) are characteristic of this text in general as an abridgement of Snorri's *Edda*,[25] and they do not imply that the scribe of U drew upon a distinct redaction of the poem. Given the nature of the alterations of the stanzas from *Vafþrúðnismál*, it is even possible that the scribe of U did not realize at these points that he was copying poetry. Similarly, there seems little reason to suppose that Snorri was working from a distinct redaction of the poem; the fact that *Gylfaginning* alone contains line 31.4–6 is scarcely conclusive. Since Snorri quotes only nine stanzas of *Vafþrúðnismál*, he may not even have had a complete copy of the poem. For that matter, we can only presume that the text of R contains the entire medieval poem, since we have no way of knowing whether the poem originally contained even more questions or a larger frame.

On the basis of the evidence – which, it must be stressed, is *very* meager – the best speculation is that Snorri was working from a lost copy of the archetype of R and A or from the archetype itself.[26] In either case R and A would themselves derive from a lost copy of the

25 Faulkes, ed., *Edda, Prologue and Gylfaginning*, by Snorri Sturluson (Oxford, New York, 1982), xxx.
26 Lindblad, "Centrala eddaproblem," 16.

archetype that accidentally omitted 31.4–6. The readings unique to the various paper manuscripts of the *Poetic Edda* (see the notes to 27.3, 31.4–6, 40, and 41.5–6) are of dubious authority, given the late date and otherwise undistinguished quality of these texts.[27]

Critical Commentary

Unlike *Vǫluspá* or *Hávamál*, which have been all but universally praised by modern readers, *Vafþrúðnismál* has met with a decidedly mixed critical reception. For some scholars, *Vafþrúðnismál* does have a stylistic excellence that renders it the equal of its predecessors in R. Finnur Jónsson, for example, regards the poem as technically excellent and praises in particular its beginning, the progress of the dialogue, and the dramatic tension that builds to the poem's conclusion. Boer, similarly, considers *Vafþrúðnismál* the most sublime Eddic poem, while Einar Ól. Sveinsson praises its language and narrative economy. But in the almost inevitable comparisons with *Vǫluspá*, *Vafþrúðnismál* is typically considered very deficient indeed. Sigurður Nordal speaks of "the swell of poetic achievement" in *Vǫluspá*, but in *Vafþrúðnismál* he sees only "a jumble of odd fragments of erudition without any proper organisation, and no attempt is made to trace the causal connection of events." In the

---

27   See further Sophus Bugge, ed., *Norrœn Fornkvæði: Islandsk Samling af folkelige Oldtidsdigte om Nordens Guder og Heroer almindelig kaldet Sæmundar Edda hins fróða* (Christiania, 1867; rpt. Oslo, 1965), xlix-lxiii. For more detailed discussion of the individual authorities, see the various facsimiles. For a survey of arguments for and against a Norwegian origin, see Finnur Jónsson, *Den oldnorske*, 54–79, and Einar Ól. Sveinsson, *Íslenzkar bokmenntir í fornöld* (Reykjavík, 1962), 188–91. For a discussion of the date of the *Edda*, see Finnur Jónsson, *Den oldnorske*, 37–54, and Stefán Einarsson, *A History of Icelandic Literature* (New York, 1957), 18–22. Lindblad ("Centrala eddaproblem") surveys Eddic scholarship in general, and Harris ("Eddic Poetry") offers detailed discussion on all the topics touched upon so far.

same vein, Hallberg observes that "in spite of occasional superb passages, poems such as *Grímnismál* and *Vafþrúðnismál* deal mostly in minute detail with questions of mythological lore without ever approaching the powerful visionary completeness of *Völuspá*."[28]

While few scholars today would claim that *Vafþrúðnismál* is the most sublime Eddic poem, it can be misleading to evaluate the poem only on the basis of comparisons. If *Vafþrúðnismál* lacks "the powerful visionary completeness" of *Vǫluspá*, this may well be because the poem makes no attempt to have such a vision. And to say this is not to reveal anything about the quality of *Vafþrúðnismál* or any other Eddic poem. To do so, I turn now to the various literary, mythological, and cultural traditions that underwrite early Norse poetry.

Composition

As with all Eddic poems, the precise way in which *Vafþrúðnismál* was composed is unknown. Earlier I noted that a tenth-century date for the earliest version implies that the poem was at first in some sense oral, since literacy did not become widespread in Iceland until after the conversion to Christianity in about the year 1000. Beyond this, much of the poem consists of language reminiscent of other oral traditions. It embodies several well-known folktale motifs, for instance.[29] But even more suggestive in this regard is the poem's dependence on formulas,

---

28 Finnur Jónsson, *Den oldnorske*, 141–42; Boer, *Die Edda*, 2: 60; Einar Ól. Sveinsson, *Íslenzkar bokmenntir í fornöld*, 275–76; Nordal, "Three Essays on *Völuspá*," trans. B.S. Benedikz and J.S. McKinnell, *Saga-Book: Viking Society for Northern Research* 18 (1970–73): 79–135, at 104; Peter Hallberg, *Old Icelandic Poetry: Eddic Lay and Skaldic Verse*, trans. Paul Schach and Sonja Lindgrenson (Lincoln, 1975), 38.

29 Maria Elena Ruggerini, "A Stylistic and Typological Approach to *Vafþrúð-nismál*," in John McKinnell and Ruggerini, *Both One and Many: Essays on Change and Variety in Late Norse Heathenism* (Rome, 1994), 139–87.

specific phrases that are used more than once in the same, or a very similar, metrical situation to express essentially the same idea. Repetition of a line within a poem is not of course peculiar to formulaic composition, for it also occurs when a refrain or incremental repetition is employed. The difference is that in certain poetic traditions the phrases and metrical shapes of formulas constitute not merely stylistic effects but also the fundamental materials by which a poem is composed.

Examples from *Vafþrúðnismál* include the three identical lines with which Óðinn begins his questions at stanzas 44, 46, 48, 50, 52, and 54, and the three identical lines at 29.1–3 and 35.1–3, which refer to the giant Bergelmir. Though the phrase in formulaic composition is relatively fixed, by nature it has the potential for substitutions that do not affect its metrical regularity. Alternation between *svinnan* and *fróþan* in Óðinn's twelve numbered questions illustrates this potential, as do the variations in the use of *inn fróþi iǫtunn*. The phrase can be combined with other lexical elements (e.g. *fyrst* [20.6] and *er sá* [35.5]), for instance, or deployed in different syntactic constructions (e.g. in 20.6 the phrase is a vocative, while in 35.5 it is the subject of a subordinate clause) to produce a metrically regular half-line. Individual phrases can also be altered through the substitution of a different adjective without affecting their metricality (e.g. *enn baldni iǫtunn* [32.5]). Even a brief examination of the rest of the *Poetic Edda* reveals that several of the formulas used in *Vafþrúðnismál*, whether one or more times, occur in other Eddic poems, and that there are other formulas that occur in two or more poems other than *Vafþrúðnismál*. The phrase *riúfaz regin* (52.6) thus also occurs (in a variety of combinations that yield a metrically regular third line in a *ljóðaháttr* strophe) at *Grm.* 4.6, *Ls.* 41.3, and *Sd.* 19.9, while *þíns um freista frama* (11.3, 13.3, 15.3, and 17.3) is closely paralleled by *síns um freista frama* (*Hv.* 2.6) and *er sá inn fróþi iǫtunn* (35.5) by *sá inn ámátki iǫtunn* (*Skm.* 10.7).

Although formulaic phrases have long been acknowledged as the building blocks of Eddic verse, their precise significance is still being debated. They certainly point to an oral background for the poems, but by themselves they say little about the nature of this orality. Were the original Eddic poems composed extemporaneously (in which case the texts that survive, like the Homeric poems, are transcriptions or later redactions) or simply memorized and recited aloud? Were the written forms always meant to be read aloud? Was there a transition from one type of composition to the other that is reflected in the poems?

In her argument that the Eddic poems are relics of ritualized drama in Scandinavia, Phillpotts identifies several qualities that she thinks indicate an origin in extemporaneous oral composition: "A characteristic almost peculiar to the chant-metre [i.e. *ljóðaháttr*] poems suggests that the period of improvisation lay not so very far behind. This is the frequency of repetition, and the linking of the strophes; devices which leave the improvising poet a moment to elaborate his question or his answer."[30] *Vafþrúðnismál* is full of the devices Phillpotts cites and is also particularly rich in formulaic language, of which I have noted only a handful of examples. More recently, the backdrop for arguments about any potentially improvisational traditions has been Milman Parry's and Albert B. Lord's studies of extemporaneous poetry in the Balkans. In this tradition, which they use as a model for interpreting the composition of the Homeric poems, an individual *guslar* ("singer") does not recite memorized poems but recreates them with every recital, with the result that specific poems may have general structural and narrative requirements but no fixed text. "The singer of tales," Lord notes, "is at once the tradition and an individual creator."[31]

---

30 Bertha S. Phillpotts, *The Elder Edda and Ancient Scandinavian Drama* (Cambridge, 1920), 93.

31 Lord, *The Singer of Tales* (Cambridge, MA, 1960; rpt. New York, 1978), 4.

While there is little cultural or literary evidence to suggest that medieval Scandinavian poets composed the way the modern Yugoslavian *guslar* does, modified versions of the Parry-Lord theory have offered helpful ways to approach the oral style of Eddic poetry. "The general trend now," Lindow observes, "is to regard eddic poems as rather like ballads, in the sense that the form is relatively fixed."[32] From this perspective, formulaic language would have primarily enabled poets to compose and recite poems (and audiences to remember them). Poems were then not made anew with every recital but were simply uttered aloud, perhaps by a special class of individuals whose job it was to preserve the ancient wisdom.[33] In Lönnroth's analysis, some variation will still naturally arise,

> not only because performers would forget or misunderstand what they had memorised (as can be seen from the many textual corruptions) but also because an oral performance will always contain *an element* of improvisation, adaptation, and individual eccentricity, even in cultures where there is a good deal of respect for tradition and insistence on correct rendering of the words handed down from older generations.[34]

In this vein, Kellogg, pointing to the fluid nature of texts in oral societies, sees Eddic poetry as culturally as well as poetically transi-

32 John Lindow, "Mythology and Mythography," in *Old Norse-Icelandic Literature: A Critical Guide*, ed. Carol J. Clover and John Lindow (Ithaca, 1985), 21–67, at 30. Also see Lars Lönnroth, "Hjálmar's Death-Song and the Delivery of Eddic Poetry," *Speculum* 46 (1971): 1–20.

33 Jan de Vries, "Om Eddaens Visdomsdigtning," *Arkiv för nordisk filologi* 50 (1934): 1–59, at 57–58.

34 Lars Lönnroth, "*Iǫrð fannz æva né upphimin.* A Formula Analysis," in *Specvlvm Norroenvm: Norse Studies in Memory of Gabriel Turville-Petre*, ed. Ursula Dronke, Guðrún P. Helgadóttir, Gerd Wolfgang Weber, and Hans Bekker-Nielsen (Odense, 1981), 310–27, at 311–12.

tional. These are poems "intended to perform the invaluable service of preserving the heart, if not the form, of a once-prosperous epic tradition," and the compiler of the Codex Regius "is clearly aware of himself ... as occupying a boundary between two worlds, his own rational, scholarly, literary world and the more fantastic world of ancient myth and legend from which the poems have come. Such an awareness is one of the organizing and cognitive habits of literacy."[35] These interpretations well account for the textual tradition of *Vafþrúðnismál*. There is variation between R and A on the one hand and the manuscripts of Snorri's *Edda* on the other, but for the most part it is on a scale that would seem to suggest minor accidental alteration during the course of recital and copying and not the ongoing oral creation of distinct redactions.

Extensive use of formulaic language and the impossibility of affixing exact dates to any of the Eddic poems make it extremely difficult to establish lines of borrowing or influence between any two poems. Some poems may in fact have directly influenced others, and in her attempt to construct a relative chronology for some of the Eddic poems, Söderberg argues that *Locasenna* shows direct borrowings from *Vafþrúðnismál*.[36] But verbal, thematic, and narrative similarities may have arisen just as easily from the shared poetic tradition. Accordingly, the formulaic similarities between *Vafþrúðnismál* and other Eddic poems that the Notes record are intended only as introductions to this intertextuality, not as evidence of influence in any direction.[37]

35 Robert Kellogg, "The Prehistory of Eddic Poetry," in *Poetry in the Scandinavian Middle Ages: The Seventh International Saga Conference* (Spoleto, 1990), 187–99, at 197.

36 Söderberg, "Formelgods och Eddakronologi."

37 For a thorough record of verbal similarities between *Vafþrúðnismál* and the rest of the *Edda,* see F. Detter and R. Heinzel, ed., *Sæmundar Edda: Mit einem Anhang* (Leipzig, 1903), 150–70, and Ruggerini, "A Stylistic and Typological Approach."

Mythological Background

If the precise nature of the orality of *Vafþrúðnismál* is thus obscure, the mythological background is far more clear. Indeed, the *Poetic Edda* and *Prose Edda* together provide a remarkably detailed picture of Norse mythology that includes the creation of the world, the activities of the gods, and the eventual demise of creation. By comparison, Old English and Old High German literatures offer only the briefest glimpses of these topics. Just when the Norse myths attained the form in which they are preserved has been yet another matter of debate, though it is reasonable to suppose that when the Northern Germanic people migrated to Scandinavia they brought with them at least the kernels of some of the stories. In a number of now classic studies, Dumézil explores several ancient and medieval mythologies with the goal of reconstructing a primitive Indo-European mythology that would have given rise to all of them.[38] *Vafþrúðnismál* in particular, Salus has argued, contains parallels with the Avestan *Gāthās;* in Yasna 44, verses 3–5, Zarathustra questions Ahura-Mazdá about the creation of the sun, moon, stars, and earth, the same topics that are the subject of verses 20–26 in the Norse poem.[39]

It is certainly possible that similar mythological motifs arose independently in different Indo-European traditions. And even if parts or the entirety of certain Norse myths did originate among the Indo-

38 For example, Georges Dumézil, *Gods of the Ancient Northmen,* ed. and trans. Einar Haugen (Berkeley, 1973).

39 Peter H. Salus, "More 'Eastern Echoes' in the *Edda*? An Addendum," *MLN: Modern Language Notes* 79 (1964): 426–28. Cf. R.I. Page, "Dumézil Revisited," *Saga-Book: Viking Society for Northern Research* 20 (1978–79): 49–69. For a valuable discussion of modern views on mythic sources and their treatment, especially in reference to Old Norse, see Margaret Clunies Ross, *Prolonged Echoes: Old Norse Myths in Medieval Northern Society* (Odense, 1994, 1998), 1: 11–41.

Europeans or their early successors, the stories nonetheless developed subsequently in a number of distinctive ways within Scandinavia. For instance, the emphasis on the Ragnarǫk, the destruction of both the heavenly and earthly realms, gives Norse mythology a tone of grim resolution (though not despair) that is absent in classical mythology. Almost certainly influenced at least in some details by Christianity, an obsession with the end of the world may have been endemic to the Germanic peoples in general, for the destruction of the world is also detailed in the ninth-century Old High German *Muspilli*, while the Old English *Beowulf* focuses in part on the rise and fall of a nation. Most of the details in *Vafþrúðnismál*, however, are peculiar to the Scandinavian tradition. Another distinctive characteristic of Scandinavian mythology is that unlike in Christianity, where God by nature is beyond reproach, the Norse gods often appear simply as supernaturally powerful humans, with all their attendant foibles. In arguing against the view that Christian poets are responsible for some of the Eddic poems, Haugen thus observes:

> In spite of the less than luminous characters possessed by some of the gods, there is no trace of the Christian view that they were demons and devils. If there are Christian influences, as in the character of Baldr, they have tolerantly been absorbed into the religion, which was not fiercely exclusive, dominated by the jealous gods of Judaism, Christianity, and Islam. Like the Greek gods of Homer and Hesiod, they could commit adultery, steal, and deceive, without losing credibility as gods.[40]

Foremost of these gods, in a variety of ways, is Óðinn, the protagonist of *Vafþrúðnismál*. He is the chief of the gods and is the god of

40 Einar Haugen, "The *Edda* as Ritual: Odin and His Masks," in *Edda: A Collection of Essays*, ed. Robert J. Glendinning and Haraldur Bessason (Manitoba, 1983), 3–24, at 3.

wisdom, poetry, and battle in particular. In Dumézil's analysis of Indo-European mythology, Óðinn embodies the magical side of "sovereignty," which Dumézil has called the god of the first function (the other side, the god of laws, is represented by Týr).[41] Óðinn is a shamanistic figure given to wandering in disguise, who spends much of his time trying to acquire knowledge by which he may avert the Ragnarǫk and his own death, both of which he knows full well to be inevitable. Medieval Christianity, as Haugen indicates, tended to regard Óðinn and the other Norse gods as devils, though in *Ynglinga Saga* Snorri Sturluson takes the less judgmental tactic of euhemerization. He explains Óðinn's connections to shape-shifting and magic by associating the god with Lappish Shamans. And by tracing Óðinn, Njǫrðr, and Freyr to Asia, Snorri offers a prehistoric explanation for how magic in general came to the north.[42]

Óðinn sacrificed one of his eyes to obtain knowledge through a drink at Mimir's well (*Vsp.* 28), and he carries with him Mimir's head for the information it provides (*Ynglinga saga* ch. 7). He hung himself on the world-tree Yggdrasill in order to obtain the runes (*Hv.* 138–9), and each day he dispatches the ravens Huginn and Muninn to gather the information of the world (*Grm.* 20). His concerns with battle and the Ragnarǫk coalesce in his supervision of the Valkyries, who choose which warriors will survive and which will die in a given battle. The

---

41 Dumézil, *Gods of the Ancient Northmen*, 26–48.

42 John Lindow, "Myth Read as History: Odin in Snorri Sturluson's *Ynglinga Saga*," in *Myth: A New Symposium*, ed. Gregory Schrempp and William Hansen (Bloomington, 2002), 107–23; and Clive Tolley, "Sources for Snorri's Depiction of Óðinn in *Ynglinga Saga*: Lappish Shamanism and the Historia Norvegiae," *Maal og Minne* (1996): 67–79. On the terror and mystery associated with Óðinn, see Lotte Motz, "Óðinn's Vision," *Maal og Minne* (1998): 11–19. Elsewhere in the medieval north, euhemerization can range from overt hostility to genial tolerance.

latter go to Valhǫll to join the *einheriar*, the champions of Óðinn who each day fight to the death and each night rise to eat and drink in celebration as they keep in training to battle on behalf of the god at the end of the world.

Despite his centrality to the entire Norse mythology, however, Óðinn generally is thought not to be native to Scandinavia, and his entrance into the Norse pantheon is judged a late development. Place-name evidence indicates that Óðinn was known (if not venerated) throughout Scandinavia, yet Turville-Petre considers "it unlikely that the cult of Óðinn, as we know it, was common among west Norse peoples before the ninth century, but it may well be that Óðinn had been the chief god of the continental Germans for many centuries." In Turville-Petre's view, Óðinn is "the god of lawlessness and, it seems, of the royal court. Such conceptions were southern in origin and hardly struck root in Norway or Iceland until heathendom was falling into its decline."[43]

So far, my discussion has not distinguished mythology from religion. And so at this point I want to consider to what extent the stories recorded in *Vafþrúðnismál* and elsewhere in the *Poetic Edda* reflect actual medieval Scandinavian religious belief and observance. Are they myths in the narrow sense – sacred narratives – or in a broader sense – traditional stories that symbolically interpret the world? If the former, was *Vafþrúðnismál,* with its accounts of the creation and destruction of the world, used in some way as part of a religious service?

There can of course be little doubt that when R and A (and even their archetype) were written, interest in the ancient gods was for the most part antiquarian, for Iceland (and indeed Norway) had been Christian for over two hundred years. But what of the tenth century,

---

43 Gabriel Turville-Petre, "The Cult of Óðinn in Iceland," in Gabriel Turville-Petre, *Nine Norse Studies* (London, 1972), 1–19, at 19 and 17. Also see H.M. Chadwick's classic *The Cult of Othin: An Essay in the Ancient Religion of the North* (London, 1899).

when *Vafþrúðnismál* was probably originally composed? Dörner has argued that as an early poem, *Vafþrúðnismál* brings together a core of an old belief with the story of Baldr; it therefore suggests that even before the advent of Christianity there was some indigenous belief in life continuing after death.[44] Such a belief might well be regarded as religious, and as I noted above, Phillpotts maintained that at least some of the Eddic poems, including *Vafþrúðnismál*, reflected an original, ritualized drama in Scandinavia. According to her theory a dialogue poem like *Vafþrúðnismál* would have been acted out in front of an audience in a quasi-religious setting, much as *Oedipus* was performed at the festival of Dionysus in ancient Greece. Arising from Sir James Frazer's work on comparative mythologies, Phillpotts's theory initially won few converts. But Haugen revived it, and in an essay devoted primarily to *Hávamál* and *Grímnismál*, which share with *Vafþrúðnismál* emphases on Óðinn and ancient history, he observes:

> I am convinced that the texts [of the Eddic poems] as we have them are very close to the cultic rituals which were enacted among them [i.e. the early Germanic tribes] as among most other archaic peoples. In emphasizing their literary quality most students have overlooked their religious values. They have found the lists of names, the so-called "wisdom poems," dry and uninteresting, because they have not penetrated behind them to the religious faith of those who composed and performed them. They have criticized the repetitiousness of some of the verses and their stereotyped form, neglecting the value of formulaic repetition in creating a mood.[45]

---

44 Hans Helmut Dörner, "Die 'Vafþrúðnismál' als Heilsbotschaft im Germanischen Heidentum," *Amsterdamer Beiträge zur älteren Germanistik* 51 (1999): 67–79. Also see John Stanley Martin, *Ragnarǫk: An Investigation into Old Norse Concepts of the Fate of the Gods* (Assen, 1972).

45 Haugen, "The *Edda* as Ritual," 21.

Yet the fact remains that there is little extra-textual evidence to indicate that a unified and codified "heathen religion" ever existed. Adam of Bremen's famous (and, significantly, late) account of the temple and sacred grove in Uppsala is a rarity in medieval Scandinavian annals. Additionally, although cultic veneration (of fertility gods, for instance) certainly took place, there is no reason to believe that the medieval North had anything similar to the established ecclesiastical and moral hierarchies of the contemporary Christian church. Rather than some kind of coherent, stable faith, indeed, Viking religious practices interacted not only with Christianity but also with a variety of non-Christian cults (as among the Lapps), with the result that they varied dynamically by time and location throughout the medieval north.[46] For reasons like these, Gunnell rejects Phillpotts's notion of ritual drama, though he has assembled evidence from literature, folklore, and cultural history to suggest the possibility that certain Eddic poems, including *Vafþrúðnismál*, may still have figured in oral performance (if not heathen ritual) of some kind.[47]

Even the impact of Christianity on the Eddic poems remains disputed, rendering judgments about pre-Christian poems and rituals all the more difficult to make. Is the story of Baldr's return, for instance, essentially pagan (as Dörner implies) or Christian? What effect did the spread of Christianity in the tenth century have on the formation and preservation of the *Edda*? Were the Eddic poems composed in reaction to Christianity, in sympathy with it, or in indifference to it? As Ross has observed, indeed, there is "no reason ... to think that this change of religion deprived traditional myths of all their truth-value."[48] In any

---

46   P.G. Foote and D.M. Wilson, *The Viking Achievement: The Society and Culture of Early Medieval Scandinavia*, 2nd ed. (London, 1980), 387–414; Thomas A. DuBois, *Nordic Religions in the Viking Age* (Philadelphia, 1999).

47   Gunnell, *The Origins of Drama in Scandinavia*.

48   Ross, *Prolonged Echoes*, 1: 18.

case, within the context of Scandinavian political instability in the thirteenth century, the impulses behind the *Poetic Edda* may be less religious sensibility than a political need to euhemerize the gods and find a
place for them in a Christian culture.[49] While the proposition that the
Eddic poems were in some sense religious is thus tantalizing, particularly in light of the poems' performative qualities, it remains a proposition that has not been widely accepted. For all these reasons, Lindow
notes, "it is speculative to regard eddic poems as myths in the narrow
sense, that is, as sacred narratives accepted as true."[50]

Whatever the religious significance of the Eddic myths and poems,
they have unquestioned significance as myths in a broader sense – as a
thriving literary tradition in medieval Scandinavia. It follows from all
that has just been said, however, that there is no reason to expect this
tradition to be coherent and unified. Rather than "correct" and "incorrect" stories, the Norse tradition has episodes and versions. This means
that while it is possible to speak of the whole of Scandinavian mythology, its unity will be more elusive, not least because mythological
systems are dynamic, not static, and the whole can change over time.[51]
If Snorri's account in *Gylfaginning* seems more coherent than that in
Vafþrúðnismál (or, indeed, *Vǫluspá*), it is because Snorri, coming late in
the literary tradition, was able to select and arrange materials from the
whole system into a mythological unity. In Martin's words, "We could
sum up Snorri's importance for mythology as being not a new source
but a richer presentation and elaboration of the older poems in the

---

49 Stefanie Würth, "Ragnarök: Götterdämmerung und Weltende in der nord-
    ischen Literatur," *Jahrbuch der Oswald von Wolkenstein Gesellschaft* 13 (2001):
    29–43; Annette Lassen, "Gud eller djævel? Kristningen af Odin," *Arkiv för
    nordisk filologi* 121 (2006): 121–38.
50 Lindow, "Mythology and Mythography," 32.
51 Andreas Heusler, *Die altgermanische Dichtung*, 2nd ed. (Darmstadt, 1957),
    189–90.

Poetic Edda."[52] The originality of Snorri's work lies in his attempt, doubtlessly inspired by the model of Christianity, to combine the various stories into a single mythological system.

In a way, *Vafþrúðnismál* may thus provide a more genuine introduction to Norse mythology than *Gylfaginning* does, for the latter is, in part, a distillation of the former. Like Snorri, the author of *Vafþrúð-nismál* may well have had an antiquarian's interest in mythology, but unlike him he did not treat his subject ironically. In *Vafþrúðnismál* as opposed to *Gylfaginning*, indeed, the various myths are not editorialized or interpreted, with the result that the poem's narrative and authorial viewpoints seem one and the same. Through this non-judgmental style and probable tenth-century origin, *Vafþrúðnismál* seems to invite an original audience for whom the poem had greater immediacy than it would have had for the audiences of Snorri's *Gylfaginning*. This being the case, some version of the poem, though not necessarily the one preserved in R, was probably extant in a time when Scandinavia was largely non-Christian.

Genre

As a contest of wits, *Vafþrúðnismál* draws on two traditions found throughout Old Norse literature. First, it shares with several Eddic poems a stress on wisdom, by which I mean both aphoristic knowledge and accumulated knowledge of history and mythology. This literary taste seems to reflect broader cultural values, for medieval Scandinavian society in general, perhaps in part because an oral culture can accumulate and transmit knowledge only through individuals, evidently valued wisdom highly. In the *Poetic Edda*, both *Vǫluspá* and *Grímnismál* offer (in part) compendia of knowledge about the creation and destruction of the

---

52 Martin, *Ragnarǫk*, 35. Also see Kurt Schier, "Zur Mythologie der *Snorra Edda*: Einige Quellenprobleme," in *Specvlvm Norroenvm*, 405–20, at 409–10.

world, while *Hávamál*, especially the early portion, contains wisdom of the aphoristic sort. Knowledge of the compendious kind – about cosmogony and eschatology – predominates in *Vafþrúðnismál*, though aphoristic knowledge occurs as well.[53]

The second widespread tradition informing *Vafþrúðnismál* is the flyting tradition, which appears in two closely related forms in medieval Scandinavian literature: the *senna* and the *mannjafnaðr*. According to Clover, the *senna* is "generally defined as a formal exchange of insults and threats and the *mannjafnaðr* [as] a formal exchange of boasts."[54] In a *senna*, individuals use insults and the wit through which they are created to engage each other in a verbal duel. A well-known late-medieval example in English is the Scots poet Dunbar's encounter with Kennedy, and in Eddic poetry perhaps the best example is *Locasenna*, in which Loki affronts most of the Norse pantheon. In a *mannjafnaðr*, which may resemble a *senna* in details and with which Beowulf's exchange with Unferth may be compared, two individuals attempt to one-up each other with boasting accounts of their own accomplishments. Perhaps the best Eddic example is *Hárbarðzlióð*, in which Óðinn, disguised as a ferryman, confronts Þorr.

The distinction between *senna* and *mannjafnaðr* is not easy to make. Adopting a structuralist perspective, Swenson suggests that *"senna* functions to establish and reaffirm a society by defining its boundaries; a *mannjafnaðr* functions to define a man's position within that society" – or, more broadly, "The *senna* constructs the hero as the subject, the 'I' of culture, and the monster as its object, the 'them' of culture; the *mannjafnaðr* establishes relationships between two subjects." But Clover,

53 See stanza 10 and note. On early Germanic wisdom literature more generally, see Carolyne Larrington, *A Store of Common Sense: Gnomic Theme and Style in Old Icelandic and Old English Wisdom Poetry* (Oxford, New York, 1993).

54 Carol J. Clover, "The Germanic Context of the Unferþ Episode," *Speculum* 55 (1980): 444–68, at 445.

noting that "neither category has a pure representative," in fact proposes that though there may have originally been a formal difference between the two types of exchange, by the time of the surviving texts both were subsumed by the general concept of flyting.[55] However *senna* and *mannjafnaðr* are classified, there are certainly many incidents in Norse literature that reflect the value medieval Scandinavian culture placed on competitions of wisdom and words. For instance, in Chapter 27 of *Ǫrvar-Odds saga*, *senna* and *mannjafnaðr* appear together when Sjólfr and Sigurðr face Oddr in a contest of insults and drinking. And a type of *mannjafnaðr* occurs as well in Chapter 10 of *Heiðreks saga*, where Óðinn, again in disguise, enters the hall of King Heiðrekr and engages the king in a riddle contest on behalf of one of the king's subjects. This episode is of special importance to the study of *Vafþrúðnismál*, for Óðinn terminates the contest with the same question with which he terminates his exchange with Vafþrúðnir (see further note at 54.4–6). More generally, not only do both Óðinn and Vafþrúðnir attempt to prove they are the wisest (as in a *mannjafnaðr*), but at least Óðinn employs the insulting language associated with the *senna* tradition (e.g. see "kaldrifiadan" at 10.6 and note).

A specialized type of the contest of wits pattern that is particularly relevant to *Vafþrúðnismál* concerns the formation of the world. Focusing on the occurrence of a specific alliterative phrase that describes the division between the heaven and the earth, Lönnroth identifies several episodes that treat creation in a parallel fashion, including the Old English *Andreas* (11.796–99), the Old High German *Wessobrunner Gebet* (1.2), the Old Saxon *Heliand* (11.2886–87), *Vǫluspá* (3.5–6), and *Vafþrúðnismál* (20.4–5). He has "set up the following tentative norm for an early Germanic treatment of the Creation theme":

55 Karen Swenson, *Performing Definitions: Two Genres of Insult in Old Norse Literature* (Columbia, SC, 1991), 56; Clover, "The Germanic Context," 445.

1. X (a mythical sage) should be challenged to tell Y about the creation.

2. X should describe the cosmic order resulting from creation as centered around the basic dichotomy "green and low earth / high heaven," expressed in the alliterative *iǫrð* / *upphiminn* formula (or a slight variant such as *eorðe* / *uprodor*).

3. Other natural elements such as the sea, mountains, trees, the sun and the moon should preferably be enumerated.[56]

The alliterative collocation *iǫrð* / *upphiminn* in fact occurs at *Vafþrúðnismál* 20.4–5, and the poem's dialogue format and thematic emphasis on cosmogony display the remaining features of the pattern Lönnroth describes. The pattern also figures in both the Eddic poem *Alvíssmál,* in which Þórr compels the dwarf Alvíss to tell him of the formation of the world, and in Snorri's *Gylfaginning,* wherein Gylfi questions Hár, Jafnhár, and Þriði in the same vein. In Lönnroth's analysis, the *iǫrð* / *upphiminn* collocation reflects a "general disposition to combine semantic elements in a certain way under certain conditions" in Germanic literature, so that the various occurrences of this phrase may have an ultimate common origin, though not necessarily any direct genetic connections with each other. The creation theme may even have influenced texts outside the Norse region, since a slight variation occurs in Runo III of the Finnish *Kalevala.* There, the semi-divine hero Väinamöinen is challenged to a contest of wits by the Lappish youth Joukahainen, who claims to have been present at, and thereby describes, the creation of the world.

The contest of wits pattern in *Vafþrúðnismál* would thus seem to root the poem firmly, though not exclusively, in medieval vernacular literary traditions. More broadly, Ellis Davidson has argued that the insults, riddles, and proverbial wisdom that pervade Norse literature are aspects of any oral tradition. She draws upon Saxo Grammaticus to suggest that riddling

---

56 Lönnroth, "*Iǫrð fannz æva né upphimin,*" 317.

contests were popular throughout twelfth-century Scandinavia in particular and that there may have been "a lively and many-sided oral tradition
flourishing in the period following the Viking Age, which has left its mark
on the poems in the *Edda*."[57] Beyond Scandinavia and oral traditions, the
format and substance of the dialogue also have similarities with what may
be a broadly Indo-European genre of didactic poetry and even with the
literature of the Latin culture of the High Middle ages. Holtsmark notes
the parallel between the contest of wits and the conversations between
masters and students found in a variety of late medieval texts. In this light,
the narrative structure of *Vafþrúðnismál* might even be interpreted as a
scholastic dialogue.[58]

The question is: Are these broader resemblances coincidental or
indicative of direct influence? Efforts to connect the *Poetic Edda* to
medieval European culture at large have not been in the main convinc-
ing, and for many scholars the poems remain consummately Norse.
Indeed, for Finnur Jónsson the form of *Vafþrúðnismál* recalls the at-
mosphere of the mead hall, where drinking-bouts, undertaken to while
away the long winter, could easily degenerate into enmity – as in fact
happens in Chapter 27 of *Ǫrvar-Odds saga*.[59] If *Vafþrúðnismál* was sub-
stantially in its present form in the tenth century, of course, any influence from later medieval culture is scarcely possible; the native
fondness for wisdom contests that Ellis Davidson has noted and scho-

57 Hilda Roderick Ellis Davidson, "Insults and Riddles in the *Edda* Poems," in
    Edda: A Collection of Essays, ed. Robert J. Glendinning and Haraldur Bessason
    (Manitoba, 1983), 25–46, at 44.

58 Anne Holtsmark, "Vafþrúðnismál," in *Kulturhistorisk Leksikon for nordisk mid-
    delalder* 19 (Copenhagen, 1975), 422–23. Also see Mary Niepokuj, "Requests
    for a Hearing in Norse and Other Indo-European Languages," *Journal of
    Indo-European Studies* 25 (1997): 49–78.

59 Finnur Jónsson, *Den oldnorske*, 143. See *Ǫrvar-Odds saga* in *Fornaldarsögur
    Norðurlanda*, ed. Guðni Jónsson (Reykjavík, 1950), 2: 310–21. More gener-
    ally see Harris, "Eddic Poetry," 106–11.

lastic interest in similar issues could simply have existed side-by-side in the twelfth and thirteenth centuries. But the indirect influence of scholastic culture on the Eddic poems as they are preserved in R would seem to be a possibility that merits further scholarly consideration.

Integrity of the Text

Scholars have identified several structural peculiarities in *Vafþrúð-nismál* that indicate that some of the stanzas in the poem as we have it were displaced early in its transmission. Some of these peculiarities were analyzed by de Vries, who regards the text of R as a compilation – a revision of an older poem to which the opening dialogue between Óðinn and Frigg was added to heighten the poem's drama and ominous tone.[60] Elsewhere de Vries describes stanzas 6–19, in which Vafþrúðnir is the questioner and Óðinn the questioned, as equally dubious for five reasons: Vafþrúðnir's concluding observation that he spoke about ancient wisdom and the Ragnarǫk with the mouth of one doomed to die (55.4–6) refers only to stanzas 20 and following; the passage in which Vafþrúðnir asks the questions is disproportionately short in comparison with the passage in which Óðinn asks; the discussion in the first nineteen stanzas is inconsistent with that in the remaining stanzas, inasmuch as stanzas 22 and 23, for instance, cover the same topic as stanzas 11 and 12; the question format in the first part is a poor imitation of that in the second; and stanza 19 in effect repeats stanza 7.[61] Citing what he sees as the poem's weak beginning, de Vries maintains that in the original version only Óðinn had asked questions and that Vafþrúð-nir's are a later addition. Whoever did this (and whenever it was done) desired most of all to demonstrate Óðinn's genius, but lacking inge-

60 De Vries, *Altnordische Literaturgeschichte*, 1: 44.
61 De Vries, "Om Eddaens Visdomsdigtning," 14–15.

nuity, the redactor could assemble only an incoherent series of questions about names. If one assumes that the beginning is a late and inadequate addition, de Vries notes, it is possible to explain 3.1–3 and *æþi þér dugi* in 4.4 as borrowings from the latter part of the poem and also the fact that Óðinn disregards Frigg's advice (i.e. the advice not to go is a late addition).

Ejder has offered codicological support for the argument that the text in R is a compilation of at least two poems.[62] He points out that rubrics introduce most of the poems in R and that *Capitulum*, which occurs before stanza 20 (see note), twice serves as a type of rubric: after stanza 25 in *Reginsmál*, where it introduces the apparently damaged conclusion, and before the prose conclusion to *Guðrúnarqviða ǫnnur*, where it may be interpreted as an introduction to *Guðrúnarqviða in þriðia*. In R, rubrics (including *Capitulum* in the two *Guðrún* poems) occur either at the beginning of the poem or, as in *Grímnismál*, at the juncture between prose and verse. In Ejder's analysis, unless *Capitulum* in *Vafþrúðnismál* is an anomaly, it, too, is a type of rubric, indicating that the scribe evidently felt that "something new" was beginning with stanza 20. Ejder, like de Vries, draws attention to the formula of stanza 4 and to the disproportion between Óðinn's questions and Vafþrúðnir's, and he concludes that though stanzas 1–19 and 20–55 were not compiled from two separate sources, the compilation is still disjointed.

Conclusive evidence about whether the text of R is a compilation might be available if A were complete. While it begins only with stanza 20 (omitting stanzas 1–19), it does so because the previous folio in the manuscript is missing, allowing for only speculation about what the folio might have contained. Nonetheless, the notion that the text of R is a compilation does have much to commend it. De Vries's arguments may be inherently subjective, resting on aesthetic assumptions about

62 Ejder, "Eddadikten," 15–17.

what constitutes good poetry in general and good Eddic poetry in particular, but Ejder's discussion begins with the codicology of R. If stanzas 1–19 were in fact grafted on to stanzas 20–55, the grafting could have been done either by the scribe of R or by the scribe of the lost archetype of all authorities.

In a complex argument Boer examines another set of possible textual defects, extending from stanza 28 to stanza 43.[63] He suggests that 35.1–3 are modeled on (hence copied from) 29.1–3 and that 35.4–6 are an addition serving to bind 35.1–3 with the question asked in 34. But this question seems out of place in a series of etiological questions. Moreover, if stanza 34 asks what is the oldest thing or creature, 31 has already answered; and if it asks about the earliest event Vafþrúðnir remembers, the subsequent questions do not follow. The question itself is inconsistent with the subjunctive in 34.3 (*vitir*), which implies that the giant might *not* know (or remember). Accordingly, Boer judges stanzas 34 and 35 as spurious.

Having removed these stanzas, Boer would then move stanzas 36–37 to a position immediately after stanza 27. He reasons that the use of *hvaðan* connects stanza 36 with stanzas 20–30, and that the subject matter of stanzas 36–37 (wind) logically follows from the subjects of stanzas 20–27: earth, sky, the moon and sun, day and night, and winter and summer. The transference of stanzas 36–37 also places stanzas 38–39 in a more logical position; with both 34–35 and 36–37 removed, 38 follows immediately after 33, and stanzas 29, 31, 33, and 38 are in fact all concerned with living beings. Boer then argues that stanzas 40–41, which are problematic in other ways (see note), are spurious, because 38.8 alludes to the gods and is thus the immediate predecessor to 42, which is also about the gods. Furthermore, stanzas 38, 39, 42, and 43

63 Boer, *Die Edda*, 2: 53–56.

offer a reasonable introduction to the remaining questions, which Óðinn asks partly in response to Vafþrúðnir's arrogance in stanza 43.

If stanzas 34 and 35 are interpolated, Boer continues, then stanza 38 is the ninth of Óðinn's questions, not the tenth. 38.2 renders stanza 38 in general even more dubious, since the future time implied by "tíva rǫc" has not yet been spoken of and since the question of 38.4–8 has nothing to do with the "tíva rǫc". The correct reading of 38.2–3, according to Boer, would be "allz þik svinnan kveða, / ef þú, Vafþrúðnir! vitir." 42.2–3 are used at 38.2–3 because with the interpolation of stanzas 34 and 35 (which results in stanza 38 being Óðinn's tenth question) stanza 38 requires alliteration on *t*. Since stanza 42 similarly requires alliteration on *t*, it follows from the preceding arguments that it originally was the tenth (*tiunda*) of Óðinn's questions. Despite their lack of thematic connection, the ill-formed stanzas 40 and 41 were invented as the eleventh question, so that stanza 42 could still alliterate on *t* (*tólfta*). Once stanzas 34 and 35 were interpolated, Boer concludes, all of the other alterations are logical results, and so Boer feels all the changes come from the same redactor. The original order of stanzas 28–43 would thus be: 36, 37, 28, 29, 30, 31, 32, 33, 38, 39, 42, 43.

Though Boer's argument seems overly ingenious, it does account for and correct a number of the structural difficulties in the poem. The thematic similarity between stanzas 36–37 and 20–27 does suggest that the former could have been displaced, and stanzas 40–41 are indeed thematically and textually aberrant. But many problems nonetheless remain with Boer's analysis. If the poet (or scribe) could normalize the problems in stanza 38 simply by incorporating 42.2–3 as 38.2–3, it would seem rather odd that to normalize stanza 42 all of stanzas 40 and 41 would have to be invented; substituting *ása* for *tíva*, for instance, would have allowed 42.2 to alliterate with *ellipta* in 42.1. Moreover, the formulaic nature of the composition of *Vafþrúðnismál* renders 35.1–3 far less problematic than Boer suggests, while stanzas 34 and 31 do not necessarily overlap semantically: the oldest incident in absolute terms need not be the oldest incident an individual remembers. And the juxtaposition of a subjunctive verb in 34.2 with indicative ones in 34.4 and 34.5 may simply be an accident of formulaic composition. The poem Boer reconstructs is in many ways superior to the poem preserved in R and A. Once stanzas 34 and 35 are accepted as interpolations, the other defects he posits are all quite possible, especially the displacement of stanzas 36 and 37. Even so, one significant problem remains: What motivated an interpolation that provides new information within the poem? If stanzas 34 and 35 are genuine, the rest of Boer's argument falls apart. The scribes of R and A, indeed, must have thought that *Vafþrúðnismál* is reasonably coherent in the form in which we have it, even if they saw stanza 20 as the beginning of a new section.

Characterization

The portrayal of character in *Vafþrúðnismál* has proved as controversial as the poem's structure. For Finnur Jónsson, at one extreme, the poet of *Vafþrúðnismál* has a knack for creating and maintaining psychologically real characters who are so life-like we can almost hear them speak. To Sigurður Nordal, at the other, the poem's framework "is an independent tale and in no way fused with the matter of the poem. Whatever speakers there might be could exchange parts, and there is no difference between Óðinn's manner of speech and Vafþrúðnir's."[64] Both assessments seem overstated. It is true enough that Óðinn and Vafþrúðnir lack the psychological depth of characters in modern fiction – the formulas and repetition of their speeches do often render them stylistically indistinguishable. But the same is of course true of most of the gods and heroes in the largely oral poetics of the *Edda*. And even if the

---

64   Finnur Jónsson, *Den oldnorske*, 142; and Nordal, "Three Essays," 103–4.

god and his adversary are not realistically drawn, the assignment of roles in the poem is far from arbitrary.

Óðinn is eminently suited to the role he plays. One of the dominant characteristics of his personality wherever he occurs in medieval Scandinavian literature is his obsession with acquiring information, and it would be out of place for Vafþrúðnir to be as desirous of information as Óðinn is. Óðinn's concealment of his identity is also characteristic of him, as is the deceit by which he wins the contest. Furthermore, his role as instigator and controller of the action of *Vafþrúðnismál* is consistent with his activities throughout the poems in the beginning of the manuscript and thereby furthers any argument for an "idea" underlying the arrangement of R. The protagonist of *Vǫluspá*, Óðinn remains the main character in the subsequent poems until *For Scírnis*, and throughout the *Edda*, it might be argued, he has his own distinctive modes of speech.[65]

By Eddic standards, Vafþrúðnir is a similarly well-motivated character. The name itself, apparently built upon *vefia* ("to fold") and *þrúðr* ("strength"), suggests "The One who Is Powerful In Tricks Or Riddles" and thus as aptly describes the giant as Gagnráþr ("The Disputant") describes Óðinn.[66] As a character, he seems intellectually limited, satisfied with merely names, even as Óðinn pursues wisdom. Indeed, while the *vǫlva* of *Vǫluspá* provides a narrative ordering for the cosmos, Vafþrúðnir can offer only a series of questions and answers.[67] And as a giant, he rep-

65 Stefán Einarsson, *A History of Icelandic Literature*, 18; Ruggerini, "A Stylistic and Typological Approach," 157-65.
66 Ejder, "Eddadikten," 5; de Vries, *Altnordisches etymologisches Wörterbuch*, 2nd ed. (Leiden, 1962), 638; Holtsmark, "Vafþrúðnismál," 423; and see the note to 8.1.
67 John McKinnell, "Late Heathen Views of the World: 1. *Vafþrúðnismál*," in McKinnell and Ruggerini, *Both One and Many*, 87–106; and Judy Quinn, "Dialogue with a *vǫlva*: *Vǫluspá*, *Baldrs draumar* and *Hyndluljóð*," in *The*

resents the major antagonists of the gods, so that the conflict in the poem is emblematic of a larger conflict in Norse mythology.

Unlike the gods, giants are forces of chaos, and the creation of the universe from the giant Ymir enacts the bringing of order out of chaos. It is because of their chaotic nature that giants seem able to live everywhere: mountains, forests, east, north. There can be harmony in such a world, but it must co-exist dynamically with the ubiquitous disorder associated with and emblemized by giants.[68] Because Óðinn's opponent is a giant, then, the poem may be a sort of actualization of the Ragnarǫk myth, in which the gods and the giants battle for the last time. In this light, stanzas 20–43 intentionally seem to exaggerate the significance of giants in the cosmos, and such exaggeration would portray Vafþrúðnir as arrogant and defiant.[69] Finnur Jónsson, indeed, describes Vafþrúðnir, in his eagerness to entrap Óðinn, as a bull blindly rushing to his doom.[70] Yet the giant is cunning as well as arrogant. In stanza 9 Vafþrúðnir attempts to lure Óðinn into his hall, and in 19.4–6 the giant springs the trap (see further below). Vafþrúðnir's character is further developed at the end of the poem, for when he discovers in stanzas 54–55 that he is the one who has in fact been caught by his own ambush, the giant responds with a solemnity and quiet dignity that befit the tone of his previous questions and answers.

Poetic Edda: Essays on Old Norse Mythology, ed. Paul Acker and Carolyne Larrington (London, 2002), 248–74, at 255.

68 Ármann Jakobsson, "Where Do the Giants Live?" *Arkiv för nordisk filologi* 121 (2006): 101–12.

69 Alv Kragerud, "De mytologiske spørsmål i Fåvnesmål," *Arkiv för nordisk filologi* 96 (1981): 9–48, at 33.

70 Finnur Jónsson, *Den oldnorske*, 142.

Structure

An account of Óðinn's journey to the giant's hall and an emphasis on cosmogony and eschatology provide narrative and thematic unity for *Vafþrúðnismál*. The initial stanzas, which de Vries and others regarded as a late addition, in fact establish both qualities and so, whatever their origin, are well-integrated with the rest of the poem. Óðinn's opening words are certainly abrupt, written in the imperative mood and presuming that the god and goddess have already heard of Vafþrúðnir's fame for wisdom. And yet any abruptness here follows from Óðinn's eagerness to acquire wisdom, which likewise provides a context for his desire to gain specific information from the giant. In effect, the poem presumes its readers know something of Eddic poetry in general, and this presumption creates the sense that *Vafþrúðnismál* begins *in medias res* and thus instantly draws the reader into the world of the poem. Moreover, Frigg's response in stanza 2 and her valediction in stanza 4 establish a somber tone that likewise continues through the remainder of the poem. Frigg even seems to know some things about the giant that escape Óðinn, for the concern she expresses is a logical response both to Vafþrúðnir's extensive wisdom and to the ruthlessness he evinces in stanza 19, when he requires that the contestants wager their heads on the outcome of the competition. In its entirety, this opening evokes an Eddic pattern in which someone about to undertake a dangerous mission discusses that mission with another before leaving home (cf. *Skm.* 1–10).

The narrative of stanza 5 shifts the action to Óðinn's entrance into Vafþrúðnir's hall (6–13), where the contest of wits proper begins, and the fact that this is a new beginning is underscored by Óðinn's use of *fyrst* in 6.4. The poet here draws upon what might be called the ritual of entrance in Norse literature. That is, many diverse texts employ an episode wherein an unexpected and unknown guest arrives in a hall and provides the inhabitants with information or engages them in a question and answer exchange. The inhabitants, in turn, receive the guest almost ceremoniously and offer food and drink to him. Such a pattern appears in *Nornagests þáttr*, where the preternatural Nornagestr arrives in the hall of King Óláfr and entertains the king and his court with ancient tales; in *Gylfaginning*, where Gylfi travels to Ásgarðr to inquire about the Æsir; and in numerous episodes in the sagas. A distinctive parallel to the ritual of entrance in *Vafþrúðnismál* that even shows verbal similarities occurs in the sixth stanza of *Locasenna*, where Loki enters Ægir's hall:

> Þyrstr ec kom   þessar hallar til,
>   Loptr, um langan veg,
> áso at biðia,   at mér einn gefi
>   mæran drycc miaðar.
> [Thirsty I, Loptr, came a long way to this hall to ask the gods
> that someone might give me a glorious drink of mead.]

This ritual of entrance, which also occurs when Beowulf arrives at Heorot, could well be a response to an unknown visitor in a preliterate culture, where guests and news of the outside world would be far more out of the ordinary than they are in an electronic or even a print culture. It is in accordance with this ritual, in any case, that Óðinn adopts the pose of a weary traveler in stanza 8 and asks for hospitality from the giant. While such a scene may be traditional, the hostility of both the god and the giant puts a narrative twist on Óðinn's entrance. By winning an invitation into Vafþrúðnir's hall, Óðinn lays a trap for the giant, even as Vafþrúðnir believes he is the one who is tricking the god into entering. As Quinn suggests, indeed, there "is a certain contrived *bonhomie* between the god and the giant as they measure each other up," which is lacking in Óðinn's encounter with the sibyl in *Vǫluspá*.[71]

71 Quinn, "Dialogue with a *vǫlva*," 257.

Stanza 11 furthers the narrative of Óðinn's decision to journey by depicting Óðinn as first speaking from the entrance to the hall and then moving into the hall itself. Such movement is central to Phillpotts's interpretation of the Eddic poems as ritualized dramas, and it does in fact give a distinctly theatrical quality to at least the first nineteen stanzas. In stanza 9 Vafþrúðnir presumably offers Óðinn a seat towards the end of the hall, and the repetition of the formula "á gólfi" ("on the floor") keeps Óðinn's physical position before the reader's eye throughout this section. Stanza 19 completes the theatrical movement of the opening. There, Vafþrúðnir offers his guest a place on the highseat beside himself, and Óðinn presumably accepts.[72] This dramatic development and the content of the poem are in fact of a piece, since Óðinn, for example, answers questions in stanzas 11 to 18 "á gólfi," and in stanzas 20 to 43 Vafþrúðnir answers questions about the cosmogony while he and the god are "í sessi saman" ("together on the seat").

While the brevity of Vafþrúðnir's questions in stanzas 11–18 may make them textually suspect, it also results in an appropriately perfunctory quality that helps account for an apparent contradiction in the poem. In 6.4–6 Óðinn implies that he is the one who will test Vafþrúðnir's knowledge, but it is in fact Vafþrúðnir who subsequently tests Óðinn; the giant himself is not tested until stanza 20. The poem may simply be structurally flawed, but within the context of the narrative Vafþrúðnir's questions do serve as a brief test of whether or not Gagnráþr is someone with whom the giant should trouble himself. A comparison could be drawn here with the Old English *Beowulf*, where Beowulf must first pass the test of Unferth, whatever or whoever motivates him, before he is allowed to confront Grendel. In this light, Vafþrúðnir's offer of a place on the highseat would in part serve as symbolic recognition of Gagnráþr's status as an equal of the giant. The competitive nature of

72 For other Norse examples of similar specificity in a hall, see Detter and Heinzel, *Sæmundar Edda*, 157.

Óðinn and Vafþrúðnir's meeting is in fact emphasized throughout this section by the formulaic repetition of *freista* and again later, in Óðinn's final series of questions, by the god's repetition of *freistaþac*.

As I noted above, the overlap between these initial questions and some of the later ones has been interpreted as an indication of their inauthenticity. But from another perspective, Vafþrúðnir's questions foreshadow what is to come in the main part of the poem. The progression from the cosmogonical questions of stanzas 11, 13, and 15 to the mythological question about Surtr in stanza 17 exactly mirrors the progression of Óðinn's questions, which move from etiological issues to the Ragnarǫk and even include a reference to Surtr's role (50). And although Vafþrúðnir asks only three questions about cosmogony, these questions and their answers provide enough information to delineate the two main cosmological distinctions: day from night, and the region of men from the region of the gods. Stanzas 20 to 43 will clarify these same distinctions. Whenever it was done, the joining of these particular questions to Óðinn's first twelve was clearly not haphazard.

Lines 1–3 of stanza 19 contains Vafþrúðnir's acceptance of Óðinn as a valid opponent (symbolized when Óðinn takes a seat beside the giant) and completes the theatrical movement of stanzas 1–19. And 19.4–6 constitutes Vafþrúðnir's acknowledgment that the contest of wits can actually begin, but only with the provision that the contestants wager their lives.[73] In two ways stanza 19 thus recapitulates the beginning of the poem and foreshadows the end. First, the pledge of heads furthers the serious, grim tone of the poem that is initiated by Frigg's warnings in the second stanza and Vafþrúðnir's threat in the seventh that his guest will not leave the hall alive unless he prove the wiser of the two; and second, *geðspeki* at 19.6 recalls "fornom stǫfom" at 1.5 and so keeps wisdom before the reader's eye as the poem's general topic. These

---

73 Cf. Finnur Jónsson, ed., *De Gamle Eddadigte* (Copenhagen, 1932), 56.

issues are picked up again in the final stanza, where Vafþrúðnir both admits that the contest will cost him his life (55.4) and affirms that the contest has been largely about "forna stafi."

Óðinn's questions are patterned in a group of twelve questions about cosmogony followed by a group of six questions about the Ragnarǫk. According to de Vries, the numerical division of these questions is not arbitrary. In his analysis, the first eighteen stanzas, the part he considered grafted on to the original poem, constitute a discrete unit consisting of an introduction and the questions of Vafþrúðnir. Stanza 19 is a transition stanza, and stanzas 20 to 55 are Óðinn's speech. Disregarding the transition stanza, there is thus a ratio of two to one in the number of stanzas between the two parts of the poem. This same ratio, of course, obtains in the eighteen stanzas in which Óðinn asks questions, and so de Vries sees a two to one ratio as one of the poem's organizing principles.[74]

Thematically centered on creation and beginning, Óðinn's first sequence of questions is structurally unified both by the three-line formula that introduces the questions and by their consecutive numbering. The latter structural device also occurs in *Hávamál* 147–62, and Ejder, pointing to the occurrence of similar numbering on the Rök Stone and in the Ten Commandments, suggests that the aim of such numbering is primarily mnemonic and pedagogical.[75] The question in stanza 20 logically begins this sequence of questions, for it concerns Ymir, the material origin of the things explored in the subsequent stanzas. The ordering of questions in this group also manifests a rationale. For example, the third question, about day and night, clearly follows from the second, about the sun and the moon. The etiological questions in these stanzas address the various parts of the cosmos primar-

74 De Vries, "Om Eddaens Visdomsdigtning," 14.
75 Ejder, "Eddadikten," 14.

ily by describing their function and not by passing judgment on them (or heathen belief) in any way. The father of the sun and the moon, which together constitute a measurement of time, is "The One who Carries Time" (23); the father of the day is "The Shining One" (25); the father of night is "The Narrow One" (25), presumably a reference to darkness; the father of winter is "The Wind-Cool One" (27); and the father of summer is "The Pleasant South" (27). From these questions about cosmogony a logical progression again leads to an account of the earth's earliest inhabitants, the giants, and then to mention of the earliest deeds of the gods – the war between the Vanir and the Æsir. The account of the giants itself furthers the poem's concerns with creation, for it, too, seems to reflect an etiological myth (see note to 29.3). By linking to Óðinn's questions through the repetition (with slight variation) of the question's last three lines, Vafþrúðnir's answers contribute to the tight structure of this first part of the exchange.

The gradual widening of the topic to the gods in stanza 38 prepares for the further widening to Valhǫll and the *einheriar* in stanzas 40 and 41, which complete Óðinn's first series of questions. Just as stanza 19 represents the structural climax of Vafþrúðnir's questions, so stanza 42 culminates the questions about cosmogony. In stanza 19, it is Vafþrúðnir who symbolically acknowledges Óðinn's wisdom, even calling him *fróþr*. In stanza 42, on the other hand, it is Óðinn who acknowledges Vafþrúðnir as wise – he calls the giant *allsvinni* – before turning to the questions about the Ragnarǫk, in which he presumably has the greatest interest. If in stanzas 11–18 Óðinn proves he is wise enough to sit beside Vafþrúðnir and question him in stanzas 20–43, in these latter stanzas Vafþrúðnir thus proves that he is wise enough for Óðinn to ask him questions about the end of time. The irony, of course, is that while Vafþrúðnir presumes he is the one who is testing and luring Óðinn, the situation is quite the opposite.

Diverging in both style and theme from his first series of questions, Óðinn's second series begins with a formula that foregrounds the gods ("fiolþ ec reynda regin") and that thereby underscores the theme of these six questions. Indeed, Óðinn's final questions all concern the Ragnarǫk and the future rather than cosmogony and the past. This is the topic that motivates many of the god's actions in Norse literature, and so the opening formula has a potentially self-revelatory quality, reflecting greater interest in the topic and, concomitantly, less desire to conceal his identity. If there is a pattern in these questions, it is not as clear as in the preceding ones, though the emphasis of stanzas 20–43 on creation and beginnings is picked up again in the references to the survivors of the Ragnarǫk (45), the continuation of the natural world (47), and the reestablishment of life in general (49) and of the gods in particular (51). As survivors of the Ragnarǫk, Óðinn's sons Víþarr and Váli offer a natural continuation of such themes, but as his children they also constitute an effective bridge to Óðinn's question about his own fate (52). The god's self-interest becomes apparent when upon learning (or confirming) the answer, Óðinn immediately loses interest in the contest. As McKinnell observes, Óðinn appears to be "more concerned about his own fate than for the survival of the world after his death."[76]

The god's final question (54) would seem to violate the implicit rules of the contest, for it concerns neither cosmogony nor eschatology and is presumably answerable only by Baldr or Óðinn himself. If Frigg's initial warnings did not trouble the god, it was perhaps because he knew that this one, unanswerable question was always at his disposal. Vafþrúðnir's resignation to his fate in the final stanza is understandable, for if Óðinn does break the rules in asking the question he does, as the

76 McKinnell, "Late Heathen Views," 103. In a related vein, Ármann Jakobsson has argued that the poem depicts Óðinn's self-interested attempt to usurp the giant's role as a father-figure. See "A Contest of Cosmic Fathers: God and Giant in *Vafþrúðnismál*," *Neophilologus* 92 (2008): 263–77.

chief of the gods he has the power and authority to do what he pleases. This resignation, moreover, is consistent with the forbidding tone that has prevailed from the opening stanzas. When Vafþrúðnir observes that he has spoken about "forna stafi" and "ragna rǫc," he not only alludes in order to the subject matter of stanzas 20–43 and 44–53 but also summarizes the entire poem, since "forna stafi" and "ragna rǫc" were the subjects of Vafþrúðnir's questions as well. In a sense, the poem ends as abruptly as it begins, for we are not told whether or how Óðinn collected his bet, and the final image of the god and the giant ominously sitting side-by-side mirrors the initial image of Frigg apprehensively confronting Óðinn.

Conclusion

Lehmann has observed that "the Eddic poems were careful compositions by highly trained poets – not rustic products of peasant conviviality."[77] The style, complexity, and artistry of *Vafþrúðnismál* fully entitle the poem, I think, to such a judgment, which comparisons to other Eddic poems can obscure. While *Vafþrúðnismál* does have a number of similarities with *Vǫluspá*, the two poems differ fundamentally in structure, narrative, and theme. To judge either one in light of the other may be to compare the proverbial apples and oranges.

Vǫluspá is a poem of doubt, both for the modern critic, who struggles to sort out its literal and figurative meanings, and for its unknown author, who evidently was neither entirely Christian nor entirely heathen. The author was, in Sigurður Nordal's view, "a divided soul which found the truth which could make it whole – but this victory appeared at the same time in poetic inspiration."[78] *Vafþrúðnismál*, conversely, is a

77 Winfred P. Lehmann, "The Composition of Eddic Verse," in *Studies in Germanic Languages and Literatures in Memory of Fred O. Nolte* (St Louis, 1963), 7–14, at 14. Also see Finnur Jónsson, *Den oldnorske*, 98–105.
78 Nordal, "Three Essays," 124.

poem of certainty. The key issue may be not whether the poem ever had any kind of religious significance, nor whether the probable allusion to the Bible in *morgindǫggvar* indicates that the poet was Christian or simply had some acquaintance with Christianity. The poem's most distinctive trait, I would argue, is that its poet apparently has conviction in what he says. If the poet was aware of a spiritual conflict in the tenth century, there is no indication of this conflict in the story, which renders as fully alive the medieval Scandinavian world that *Vǫluspá* describes as passing away.

Strictly speaking, as Ejder points out, *Vafþrúðnismál* is neither a *mannjafnaðr* nor a *senna*.[79] Yet it might still be called quintessentially Norse in the traditions it draws upon: the wisdom contest, the ritual of entrance, the conflict between gods and giants, and the character of Óðinn. The poem's structural peculiarities have led readers to approach *Vafþrúðnismál* as a compilation and therefore to emphasize the coherence of only individual parts. De Vries, for instance, characterizes Vafþrúðnir's knowledge as limited to a disjointed series of mythological facts and Óðinn's as more broadly focused on the world's organic connections. Finnur Jónsson, similarly, contrasts Óðinn's genuine wisdom and intellectual vision, delivered in an elegantly calm voice, with Vafþrúðnir's self-confidence, intellectual inflexibility, and sterile command of past and future events.[80] Both analyses account very well for the differences between the two characters and the two major parts of the poem (stanzas 1–18 and 20–55), but the ways in which these two parts complement each other in the overall effect of the poem should also be considered. Whatever the scribe of R intended by *Capitulum*, indeed, several narrative and thematic unities govern the poem in its entirety.

79 Ejder, "Eddadikten," 7.
80 De Vries, *Altnordische Literaturgeschichte*, 43; Finnur Jónsson, *Den oldnorske*, 142.

At a narrative level, the poem tells a tense, though generally not sus-penseful, story. Indeed, suspense was clearly of little concern to the poet, for the audience knows from the first who Gagnráþr is and, consequent-ly, that (but not necessarily how) he will win the contest. As McKinnell notes, since Vafþrúðnir can win the contest only by "unmasking the true identity of his visitor," whatever suspense the poem has lies in the uncertainty of whether this will happen before the giant, who receives several hints about who his visitor is, determines his identity.[81]

The characters who inhabit the poem are well-suited to this narrative, with *Vafþrúðnismál* displaying the essence of Óðinn: wise, crafty, and, perhaps only in light of these qualities, courageous. The god is bold enough to disregard Frigg's admonition and visit Vaf-þrúðnir, and wise enough to answer the giant's questions. But it is Óðinn's deceit that may embolden him, for he knows that he has one question that guarantees him victory. The ominous tone of the poem's opening is intensified with the wager made in stanza 19, though there is irony in Vafþrúðnir's offer of a seat beside himself; while the giant may think that in doing so he is trapping his unexpected guest, it is the giant himself who will be trapped by Óðinn's calculation. The ques-tions asked by Óðinn increase the tension of the poem, because the reader (or original audience) familiar with the god's duplicity expects from the first not only that he will win the contest but that victory will come through deceit. The climax of the poem in stanza 54 is fittingly ironic. While the giant, perhaps already suspicious of his guest's iden-tity, discusses the Ragnarøk, he finds that he has been participating in and in fact helping to create his own personal destruction.

Thematically, *Vafþrúðnismál* would at first seem problematic. Why would Óðinn bother to ask most of the questions he does, since he presumably already knows a great deal about "forna stafi" and "ragna

81 McKinnell, "Late Heathen Views," 101.

rǫc"? Indeed, in *Grímnismál* the god declares much of the wisdom of which he feigns ignorance in *Vafþrúðnismál*. The answer might be simple malice or a larger "idea" in R, by which *Grímnismál* is a sort of sequel to *Vafþrúðnismál*. Within the context of Norse representations of Óðinn, a more likely answer begins with the question he asks in stanza 52.3, for his own salvation and the acquisition of wisdom are his most prominent interests throughout Norse mythology. As I suggested earlier, Óðinn very likely knows the answer to even this question, and so his motivation in the narrative (if a psychological cause needs to be identified) may be only to confirm what he has heard elsewhere. As Quinn archly observes, *Vǫluspá* suggests that when Óðinn "wanted to hear the whole story, rather than answers to quiz questions, he went directly" to a prophetess.[82] But if a simple desire to confirm his own fate is in fact what motives the god, the preceding questions of both Óðinn and Vafþrúðnir might seem to be an unintegrated and unnecessarily long prelude. It is at the thematic level that the purpose of these questions may be the most accessible.

Jón Helgason sees *Vafþrúðnismál* as primarily a compendium of mythological knowledge, written by a poet who was himself interested in what myths can reveal about experience.[83] Indeed, in its cosmological, divine, and eschatological topics, *Vafþrúðnismál* sketches the physical and metaphysical outline of the medieval Scandinavian world. Not only does the poem demarcate the structure of the cosmos, but, in the character of Óðinn, it affirms the medieval Scandinavian values of heroism, wit, and courage. In effect, *Vafþrúðnismál* emblematizes the attitude as well as the structure of the Norse experience. For McKinnell, thus, the poem ultimately tests "whether Fate is as immutable as it seems," and in so doing envisions an amoral post-Ragnarǫk world in which "the things which

82 Quinn, "Dialogue with a *vǫlva*," 256.

83 Jón Helgason, "Norges og Islands Digtning," 33.

will ensure survival are nature, the stubborn will to live in human beings, and on the highest level courage, strength and the taking of just revenge for one's close relatives."[84]

As challenging as such a vision may be, it is not a pessimistic one, concerned with the dissolution of society and belief, for the topics of the poem are thematically unified by an emphasis on births and beginnings – the earth's, the sun's and the giants'. Even the account of the Ragnarǫk develops this theme, since the questions Óðinn asks are primarily concerned with what will survive and begin again after the final battle, not with what will perish in it. Indeed, as Larrington observes, if the poem mimics the Ragnarǫk (resulting in only "a temporary triumph for Óðinn"), it also suggests that the future "may unfold promisingly as humans and gods begin a new history together."[85] Vǫluspá also treats the rebirth of the world, of course, but it does not share with Vafþrúðnismál a consistent thematic emphasis on life and rejuvenation. While in narrative terms, then, Vafþrúðnismál tells of the time Óðinn visited Vafþrúðnir in the vain hope of finding a way to avert his death, in thematic terms the poem defines and sustains the values and dimensions of the world in which it was produced. Vafþrúðnismál is thus both entertaining narrative and, from the perspective of the "Creation theme," a heuristic device for its medieval audience.[86]

---

84 McKinnell, "Late Heathen Views," 102, 106.

85 Carolyne Larrington, "Vafþrúðnismál and Grímnismál: Cosmic History, Cosmic Geography," in The Poetic Edda: Essays on Old Norse Mythology, ed. Paul Acker and Carolyne Larrington (London, 2002), 62–77, at 68.

86 For discussions of the senna and mannjafnaðr traditions, see Clover, "The Germanic Context," and "Hárbarðsljóð as Generic Farce," Scandinavian Studies 51 (1979): 124–45, and also Marcel Bax and Tineke Padmos, "Two Types of Verbal Dueling in Old Icelandic: The Interactional Structure of the senna and the mannjafnaðr in Hárbarðsljóð," Scandinavian Studies 55 (1983): 149–74. For a discussion of Norse cosmogony and cosmology that uses the Eddic poems as a

Meter

Eddic poetry was composed in varieties of the four stress long line common throughout early Germanic verse. The primary metrical unit is the half-line, but because of the alliterative linking between half-lines the whole line is typically the basis of discussion. The meter used in most of the narrative Eddic poems (e.g. *Atlaqviða*) is *fornyrðislag* ("old story meter"), in which each half-line has two stressed syllables surrounded by a varying number of unstressed syllables (the stressed syllables are also called lifts, and the unstressed ones sinkings). The first stressed syllable of the second half-line generally alliterates with one or both of the stressed syllables in the first half-line.

point of departure, see John Stanley Martin, "*Ár vas alda*. Ancient Scandinavian Creation Myths Reconsidered," in *Specvlvm Norroenvm*, 357–69; and for an examination of Norse mythology in general see Lindow, "Mythology and Mythography." Ross (*A History of Old Norse Poetry and Poetics* [Cambridge, New York, 2005]) offers a thorough overview of all Norse poetry, skaldic and Eddic, surveying critical issues, manuscripts, metrics, and meta-poetic commentaries like the grammatical treaties and Snorri's *Edda*, and Heather O'Donoghue (*From Asgard to Valhalla: The Remarkable History of the Norse Myths* [London, 2007]) surveys the range of Norse myths along with their post-medieval reception and use. Lindow's *Handbook of Norse Mythology* (Santa Barbara, CA, 2001) contains brief essays on the deities, themes, and concepts of Norse mythology. For discussions of Óðinn see de Vries, *Altgermanische Religionsgeschichte*, 2nd ed. (Berlin, 1956–57), 27–106; Ellis Davidson, *Gods and Myths of Northern Europe* (Harmondsworth, Baltimore, 1964), 48–72; Turville-Petre, *Myth and Religion*, 35–74; and Kris Kershaw, *The One-Eyed God: Odin and the (Indo-) Germanic Männerbünde* (Washington, DC, 2000). Motz ("Gods and Demons of the Wilderness: A Study in Norse Tradition," *Arkiv för nordisk filologi* 99 [1984]: 175–87) discusses the origin and function of giants in Norse literature, and Axel Olrik (*Om Ragnarok* [Copenhagen, 1902–14]) is a still useful consideration of the Ragnarǫk. For the latter also see Martin, *Ragnarǫk*. Harris ("Eddic Poetry") is again especially valuable on all these topics, as well as on the orality of the Eddic poems.

Vafþrúðnismál is written in *ljóðaháttr* ("chant meter"), wherein a whole line on the pattern of *fornyrðislag* is followed by a shorter one consisting of two (e.g. 22.6) or three (e.g. 9.6) stresses. In this third line (known as the Full Line) there is no caesura (the palpable pause after a half-line that is typically indicated in modern editions by a space), and the stressed syllables alliterate only with each other, not with those in the adjoining lines. Eddic poetry, unlike Old English poetry, is strophic, and a strophe of *ljóðaháttr* consists of two occurrences of the pattern two half-lines and a third line. As is the case throughout the Norse poetic tradition, however, this strophe has variations: an extra *fornyrðislag* line can be added (see 38.4–7), or an extra Full line, either in the middle of a strophe (43.3–4) or at the end (42.6–7). An extra half-stanza can also be added (55.7–9).

Ljóðaháttr clearly has a great deal of flexibility inherent in it. Indeed, given the vagaries of manuscript transmission, in which texts were copied margin to margin without divisions of lines or stanzas, metrical regularity could sometimes be more conceptual than actual – more of an expectation a reader brought to a text than a specific property of that text.[87] In *Vafþrúðnismál* in particular, several initial unstressed syllables are permissible, especially in the second half-line (e.g. 11.2). Moreover, the same word in the same metrical position can alliterate or not depending on how the poet completes the line (see the use of *Segðu* in stanzas 20 and following). Other peculiarities are characteristic of *ljóðaháttr* in general. For instance, the conclusion of the Full Line typically does not involve a long accented syllable followed by a short unaccented one, which is the most common stress-pattern in Eddic verse; rather the Full Line generally concludes with some type of metrical resolution. In *iǫtun* (1.6), for example, the accented syllable is short, while in *mari* (12.6) two short syllables are the equivalent of one long one.

---

87 T.W. Machan, "Alliteration and the Editing of Eddic Poetry," *Scandinavian Studies* 64 (1992): 216–27.

The rationale behind some of the features of *ljóðaháttr* is so uncertain that Turville-Petre has described it as "the most puzzling and one of the most interesting of Norse measures."[88] The nature of the Eddic poems written in *ljóðaháttr* would seem to be significant, for they all involve significant portions of dialogue and almost all of them, Phillpotts points out, "are careful to impart mythological information."[89] Phillpotts, again, sees the *ljóðaháttr* poems in particular as relics of a ritualized drama in early Scandinavia. Martin further proposes, "The word *ljóð* in *ljóðaháttr* ... could suggest either a sacred origin or the limitation of a once more general metre to sacred use." Since "artistic influence" is always a possibility, however, "It is preferable to imagine poets composing in a tradition established by seasonal festivals or by an heroic society or tradition, themselves unconscious of its origin."[90] Though the ritualized drama theory is not widely in favor today, it is intriguing that poems as stylistically and thematically similar as *Hávamál*, *Vafþrúðnismál*, and *Grímnismál* should all be composed in *ljóðaháttr*. The significance of the meter could be profitably explored.[91]

The Present Edition

This edition of *Vafþrúðnismál* has been prepared from facsimile editions of the various authorities. The base manuscript is R, for this manuscript contains the only apparently complete text of the poem. Emendations, both conjectural and based on the readings of other

---

88 Gabriel Turville-Petre, *Scaldic Poetry* (Oxford, 1976), xvi.
89 Phillpotts, *The Elder Edda*, 47.
90 Martin, *Ragnarǫk*, 27–28.
91 For further discussion see Sijmons, *Die Lieder: Text*, ccxxxvii–ccxliii; L. Läffler, "Om några underarter av Ljóðaháttr," *Studier i nordisk filologi* 4 (1913): 1–124; Finnur Jónsson, *Den oldnorske*, 105–11; and Gunnell, *The Origins of Scandinavian Drama*, 185–94.

authorities, are enclosed in square brackets. I have collated the text of R with that of A and with the selections found in R², T, U, and W. Substantive variants appear in the Textual Notes. I have not collated the various late paper manuscripts, for which the interested student should consult Bugge's 1867 edition. The arrangement of the lines, punctuation, and diacritics are my own; the text of R is written straight across the page without line divisions (as is usual in early medieval manuscripts), and punctuation and diacritics appear only sporadically. All standard abbreviations have been expanded silently.

This edition preserves much more of the orthography of R than have most previous editions of Eddic poetry. I have adopted this procedure in accordance both with the general aim of this edition – to introduce students to Eddic poetry – and with the modern scholarly emphasis on preserving the integrity of medieval texts. Accordingly, while the advanced scholar may at first be discomfited by forms like *hvaþan* (20.4) and *veitzst* (34.5), the beginning student will come to recognize through them the representational diversity that characterizes medieval literature but that is often concealed, especially for Old Norse texts, by regularization.

A strictly diplomatic presentation of vowels in particular can cause needless and sometimes (for the beginning student) unsolvable problems of interpretation, however, and so I have followed Dronke's procedures in *The Poetic Edda* for the present edition. Specifically, I have made the following regularizations when appropriate:

ǫ́, o appear as ǫ
ǫ appears as œ
ę, e appear as æ, e
o, ǫ appear as ø

Though there is thus some inconsistency in the present procedure, it is far less than appears in many Norse editions, where þ and ð, for instance, are regularized, but *c* and *k* are not. I have followed the present procedure specifically as a way of introducing the difficulties of Eddic poetry without rendering the language so difficult as to be obscure and, finally, uninviting.

The orthographic diversity and peculiarities of manuscript Eddic poetry stem from two general causes: the medieval uncertainty and inconsistency in adapting Roman spelling to the Norse language, and changes in the Norse language throughout the medieval period. The following guidelines may help students who have begun Norse studies with the regularized texts of Gordon, Turville-Petre, or Barnes.

1.   There is a great deal of interchange between the graphs ð, þ, and *d*. Where regularized texts read ð, Eddic poems very often read þ (e.g. *áþr*, 29.2); *d* also occasionally appears where one would expect ð (e.g. *hvadan*, 22.4). Less frequently, ð appears where þ is expected (e.g. *ðau*, 45.5), and þ where *t* is expected (e.g. *iþ*, 24.1). These variations are due both to medieval Norse sound changes and to the unsystematic attempts to represent in Norse the voiced and voiceless dental fricatives, which are absent in Latin and thus had no fixed representation in the Roman alphabet.[92]

2.   *c* often appears where one would expect *k* (e.g. *ec*, 3.1), but the latter form does appear in *Vafþrúðnismál* (e.g. *koma*, 37.5). The graph *k* was very rare in Latin writing, and the origin and date of its introduction to Germanic writing are still a matter of debate. In any event, in both Old Norse and late Old English texts *k* was often used for the palatal voiceless stop (e.g. OE *kéne*, ON *kind*), and *c* for the velar voiceless stop (e.g. OE *cunnan*, ON *coma*); in OE editions the graph *c* is typically generalized, while in ON ones *k* is typically so used. Early manuscripts like R also use *qv* where *kv* is expected (e.g. *qveþa*, 24.2).[93]

92   Noreen, *Altnordische Grammatik*, §§ 35, 44, 238, 248.
93   Noreen, *Altnordische Grammatik,* §39.

3. *i* appears where either *i* or *j* is expected; the latter graph was generalized in the early modern period as a way of distinguishing the glide from the vowel.[94]

4. The unstressed high front vowel can be represented by *e* rather than *i*, although *Vafþrúðnismál* has only a few examples (e.g. *enn*, 32.5).[95]

5. The unstressed back mid to high inflectional vowel in, for instance, third person plural preterite verbs or noun and adjective dative plurals is *o*, not *u* (e.g. *qváþo*, 33.2, *sonom*, 15.5). /u/ is in fact the historical vowel (cf. Gothic *qéþum*, *sunum*), but early in the Norse period this vowel acquired a quality represented by *o;* after 1300 /u/ arose again independently.[96]

It is worth underscoring here that the Eddic forms are *not* corruptions of the forms found in most editions. The latter are regularizations of the former. If the manuscripts of the relevant texts are examined, orthographic diversity similar to that found in R and preserved here underlies the regularized texts.

I also want to note that this edition does not attempt to recover the lost archetype from which the various authorities descend. The manuscripts themselves are our only reliable witnesses to how medieval literature existed, and without a critical apparatus medieval readers often would not have known that the text they were reading contained "scribal contaminations." In a very real sense the author of the *Poetic Edda* is not whoever originally composed the poems but whoever collected and presented the versions found in the Codex Regius and in AM 748 I 4to. If modern readers are to recover and appreciate medieval meanings, the integrity of the manuscripts needs to be respected.

---

94 Noreen, *Altnordische Grammatik*, §25.
95 Noreen, *Altnordische Grammatik*, §149.1.
96 Noreen, *Altnordische Grammatik*, §146.1.

Accordingly, R has been emended only when the sense of the passage requires emendation. Problematic but intelligible passages, including some in which the alliteration has been damaged, are left alone, though the notes offer clarification.

In general, the objective of the Explanatory Notes is to aid the student in translating and interpreting the poem and thereby, I hope, to indicate some of the linguistic and literary characteristics of Eddic poetry. Cross-references to other Norse texts are included, as are the comments of previous scholars. The student is simply directed to extended discussions when they fall outside the scope of this edition. In difficult passages, the Notes generally attempt to explain the nature of the problem and to provide several possible solutions rather than to assert a definitive one. Eddic poems are referred to by stanza or stanza and line number and are quoted from Neckel's edition. *Ynglinga saga* and *Gylfaginning* are cited by chapter number; quotations of the former are taken from Wessén's edition and of the latter from Faulkes's.

Vafþrúðnismál

1. "Ráþ þú mér nú, Frigg,   allz mic fara tíðir
       at vitia Vafðrúdnis;
    forvitni micla   qveþ ec mér á fornom stǫfom
       við þann inn alsvinna iǫtun."

2. "Heima letia   ek munda Heriafǫðr
       í gǫrðom goða,
    þvíat engi iǫtun   ec hugða iafnramman
       sem Vafðrúðni vera."

3. "Fiǫlþ ec fór,   fiǫlþ ec freistaða,
       fiǫlþ ec reynda regin;
    hitt vil ec vita –   hvé Vafðrúþnis
       salakynni sé."

4. "Heill þú farir,   heill þú aptr komir,
       heill þú á sinnom sér!
    œþi þér dugi,   hvars þú scalt, Aldafǫþr,
       orðom mæla iǫtun."

5. Fór þá Óðinn   at freista orþspeci
       þess ins alsvinna iǫtuns.
    At hǫllo hann com   oc átti Íms faðir;
       inn gecc Yggr þegar.

6. "Heill þú nú, Vafðrúðnir!   Nú em ec í hǫll komin[n]
       á þic siálfan siá.
    Hitt vil ec fyrst vita,   ef þú fróþr sér
       eþa alsviþr, iǫtunn."

7.   "Hvat er þat manna   er í mínom sal
          verpomc orði á?
      Út þú né comir   órom hǫllom frá,
          nema þú inn snotrari sér."

8.   "Gagnráþr ec heiti;   nú emc af gǫngo kominn
          þyrstr til þinna sala;
      laðar þurfi   hefi ec lengi farit
          oc þinna andfanga, iǫtunn."

9.   "Hví þú þá, Gagnráþr,   mæliz af gólfi fyrir?
          Farþu í sess í sal!
      Þá scal freista   hvárr fleira viti,
          gestr eþa inn gamli þulr."

10.   "Óauþigr maþr   er til auþigs kømr,
          mæli þarft eþa þegi;
      ofrmælgi micil   hygg ec at illa geti,
          hveim er viþ kaldrifiadan kømr."

11.   "Segþu, mér, Gagnráþr,   allz þú á gólfi vill
          þíns um freista frama,
      hvé sá hestr heitir   er hverian dregr
          dag o[f] dróttmǫgo."

12.   "Scinfaxi heitir,   er inn scíra dregr
          dag um dróttmǫgo;
      hesta beztr   þyccir hann meþ Reiðgotom,
          ey lýsir mǫn af mari."

13. "Segdu þat, Gagnráþr, allz þú á gólfi vill
    þíns um freista frama,
  hvé sá iór heitir er austan dregr
    nótt o[f] nýt regin."

14. "Hrímfaxi heitir, er hveria dregr
    nótt o[f] nýt regin;
  méldropa fellir hann morgin hvern
    þaðan kømr dǫgg um dala."

15. "Segðu þat, Gagnráþr allz þú á gólfi vill
    þíns um freista frama,
  hvé sú á heitir er deilir meþ iǫtna sonom
    grund oc meþ goðom."

16. "Ífing heitir á, er deilir meþ iǫtna sonom
    grund oc meþ goðom;
  opin renna hon scal um aldrdaga,
    verþrat íss á á."

17. "Segðu þat, Gagnráþr, allz þú á gólfi vill
    þíns um freista frama,
  hvé sá vǫllr heitir er finnaz vígi at
    Surtr oc in sváso goð."

    Óðinn qvaþ:
18. "Vígríþr heitir vǫllr, er finnaz vígi at
    Surtr oc in sváso goð;
  hundraþ rasta hann er á hverian veg –
    sá er þeim vǫllr vitaþr."

Vafþrúðnir qvaþ:

19. "Fróþr ertu nú, gestr!   Far þú á becc iǫtuns,
        oc mælomc í sessi saman!
     Hǫfði veðia   við scolom hǫllo í,
        gestr, um geðspeki."

Capitulum

Óðinn qvaþ:

20. "Segðu þat iþ eina,   ef þitt œþi dugir,
        oc þú, Vafþrúðnir, vitir,
     hvaþan iǫrð um com   eþa uphimin[n]
        fyrst, inn fróþi iǫtunn."

Vafþrúðnir qvaþ:

21. "Ór Ymis holdi   var iǫrð um scǫpuð,
        en ór beinom biǫrg;
     himinn ór hausi   ins hrímkalda iǫtuns,
        enn ór sveita siór."

Óðinn qvaþ:

22. "Segðu þat annat,   ef þitt œþi dugir,
        oc þú, Vafþrúðnir, vitir,
     hvadan máni um kom,   svá at ferr menn yfir,
        eþa sól iþ sama."

Vafþrúðnir qvaþ:

23. "Mundilfœri heitir,   hann er mána faþir,
        oc svá sólar iþ sama;
     himin hverfa   þau scolo hverian dag
        ǫldom at ártali."

Óðinn qvaþ:

24. "Segðu þat iþ þriðia,   allz þic svinnan qveþa,
        oc þú, Vafþrúðnir, vitir,
    hvaðan dagr um com   – sá er ferr drót[t] yfir –
        eþa nótt meþ niðom."

Vafþrúðnir qvaþ:

25. "Dellingr heitir,   hann er dags faþir,
        enn nót[t] var Nǫrvi borin;
    ný oc niþ   scópo nýt regin,
        ǫldom at ártali."

Óðinn qvaþ:

26. "Segðu þat iþ fiórða,   allz þic fróþan qveþa,
        oc þú, Vafþrúðnir, vitir,
    hvaðan vetr um com   eþa varmt sumar
        fyrst meþ fróþ regin."

Vafþrúðnir qvaþ:

27. "Vindsvalr heitir,   hann er vetrar faþir,
        enn Svásuþr sumars."

Óðinn qvaþ:

28. "Segdu þat iþ fimta,   allz þic fróþan qveþa,
        oc þú, Vafþrúðnir, vitir,
    hverr ása ellztr   eþa Ymis niðia
        yrþi í árdaga."

Vafþrúðnir qvaþ:

29. "Ørófi vetra   áþr væri iorþ scopuþ
　　　þá var Bergelmir borinn;
　　Þrúdgelmir   var þess faðir,
　　　enn Aurgelmir afi."

Óðinn qvaþ:

30. "Segðu þat iþ sétta,   allz þic svinnan qveþa,
　　　oc þú, Vafþrúðnir, vitir,
　　hvaþan Aurgelmir   com meþ iotna sonom
　　　fyrst, in[n] fróþi iotunn."

Vafþrúðnir qvaþ:

31. "Ór Élivágom   stucco eitrdropar;
　　　svá óx unz varð ór iotunn.
　　[Þar órar ættir   kómu allar saman,
　　　því er þat æ allt til atalt.]"

Óðinn qvaþ:

32. "Segðu þat iþ siaunda,   allz þic svinnan qveþa,
　　　oc þú, Vafþrúðnir, vitir,
　　hvé sá born gat,   enn [b]aldni iotunn,
　　　er hann hafdit gýgiar gaman."

Vafþrúðnir qvaþ:

33. "Undir hendi vaxa   qváþo hrímþursi
　　　mey oc mog saman;
　　fótr við fœti   gat ins fróða iotuns
　　　se[x]hofðaþan son."

Óðinn qvaþ:

34. "Segðu þat iþ átta,   allz þic fróþan qveþa,
    oc þú, Vafþrúðnir, vitir,
  hvat þú fyrst mant   eþa fremst um veitzst –
    þú ert alsviþr, iǫtunn."

Vafþrúðnir qvaþ:

35. "Ørófi vetra   áþr væri iǫrð um scǫpuð,
    þá var Bergelmir borinn;
  þat ec fyrst um man,   er sá inn fróþi iǫtunn
    var á lúðr um lagiðr."

Óðinn qvaþ:

36. "Segðu þat iþ níunda,   allz þic svinnan qveþa,
    [oc] þú, Vafþrúðnir, vitir,
  hvadan vindr um kømr,   svá at ferr vág yfir –
    æ menn hann siálfan um siá."

Vafþrúðnir qvaþ:

37. "Hræsvelgr heitir,   er sitr á himins enda,
    iǫtunn í arnar ham;
  af han[s] vængiom   qveþa vind koma
    alla menn yfir."

Óðinn qvaþ:

38. "Segðu þat iþ tíunda,   allz þú tíva rǫc
    ǫll, Vafðrúðnir, vitir,
  hvaðan Niǫrðr um kom   með ása sonom;
  hofom oc hǫrgom   hann ræðr hunnmǫrgom,
    oc varþaþ hann ásom alinn."

Vafþrúðnir qvaþ:

39. "Í Vanaheimi   scópo hann vís regin
       oc seldo at gíslingo goðum;
       í aldar rǫc   hann mun aptr coma
       heim meþ vísom vǫnom."

Óðinn qvaþ:

40. "Segðu þat et ellipta,   hvar ýtar túnom í
       hǫggvaz hverian dag."

Vafþrúðnir qvaþ:

41. "[Allir einheriar   Oðins túnum í
       hǫggvaz hverian dag;]
       val þeir kiósa   oc ríþa vígi frá —
       sitia meirr um sáttir saman."

Óðinn qvaþ:

42. "Segþu þat iþ tólfta,   hví þú tíva rǫc
       ǫll, Vafðrúðnir, vitir;
       frá iǫtna rúnom   oc allra goða
       segir þú iþ sannasta,
       inn allsvinni iǫtunn."

Vafþrúðnir qvaþ:

43. "Frá iǫtna rúnom   oc allra goða
       ec kann segia satt,
       þvíat hvern hefi ec heim um komit;
       nío kom ec heima   fyr Niflhel neðan,
       hinig deyia ór helio halir."

Óðinn qvaþ:

44. "Fiǫlþ ec fór,   fiǫlþ ec freistaþac,
        fiǫlþ ec reynda regin:
     hvat lifir manna,   þá er inn mæra líþr
        Fimbulvetr meþ firom?"

Vafþrúðnir qvaþ:

45. "Líf oc Lífðrasir –   enn þau leynaz muno
        í holti Hoddmimis;
     morgindǫggvar   ðau sér at mat hafa,
        þaðan af aldir alaz."

Óðinn qvaþ:

46. "Fiǫlþ ec fór,   fiǫlþ ec freistaþac,
        fiǫlþ ec reynda regin:
     hvaðan cømr sól   á inn slétta himin,
        þá er þessa hefir Fenrir farit?"

Vafþrúðnir qvaþ:

47. "Eina dóttur   berr Alfrǫðull,
        áþr hana Fenrir fari;
     sú scal ríða,   þá er regin deyia,
        módur brautir mær."

Óðinn qvaþ:

48. "Fiǫlþ ec fór,   fiǫlþ ec freistaþac,
        fiǫlþ ec reynda regin:
     hveriar ro þær meyiar   er líþa mar yfir,
        fródgediaþar fara?"

Vafþrúðnir qvaþ:

49. "Þriár þióðar   falla þorp yfir
      meyia Mǫgþrasis;
      hamingior einar   þeira í heimi ero
      þó þær meþ iǫtnom alaz."

Óðinn qvaþ:

50. "Fiǫlþ ec fór,   fiǫlþ ec freistaþac,
      fiǫlþ ec reynda regin:
      hverir ráþa æsir   eignom goða,
      þá er slocnar Surtalogi?"

Vafþrúðnir qvaþ:

51. "Víþarr oc Váli   byggia vé goða,
      þá er slocnar Surtalogi;
      Móþi oc Magni   scolo Miǫllni hafa
      oc vinna at vígþroti."

Óðinn qvaþ:

52. "Fiǫlþ ec fór,   fiǫlþ ec freistaþac,
      fiǫlþ ec reynda regin:
      hvat verþr Óðni   at aldrlagi,
      þá er riúfaz regin?"

Vafþrúðnir qvaþ:

53. "Úlfr gleypa   mun Aldafǫþr,
      þess mun Víþarr reca;
      kalda kiapta   hann klyfia mun
      vi[t]nis vígi at."

Óðinn qvaþ:

54. "Fiǫlþ ec fór,   fiǫlþ ec freistaþac,
       fiǫlþ ec reynda regin:
     hvat mælti Óðinn,   áþr á bál stigi,
       siálfr í eyra syni?"

Vafþrúðnir qvaþ:

55. "Ey manne þat veit,   hvat þú í árdaga
       sagdir í eyra syni.
     Feigom munni   mælta ec mína forna stafi
       oc um ragna rǫc:
     nú ec viþ Óðin   deildac mína orþspeci —
       þú ert æ vísastr vera."

TEXTUAL NOTES

2.5 iafnramman] iafnrammann R

4.5 scalt] s. or R

6.2 kominn] komin R

11.6 of] oc R

13.6 of] oc R

14.3 of] oc R

14.4 méldropa] mel dropa R

18.5 hverian] hvern T

18.6 vǫllr] v. of T

20.3 oc] æ A (abbreviation for eða)

20.5 uphiminn] up himin R; upp himinn A

22.4 um] of A

22.5 svá at] sa ær A

23.1 Mundilfœri] Mundilfæri A

24.3 oc] æ A

24.5 drótt] drot R

25.1 Dellingr] Dællingr A

25.3 nótt] not R

26.6 með] um A

29.2 iǫrþ] i. um A

30.2 svinnan] froðan A

30.4–6 hvaþan ... iǫtunn] om. U

30.6 inn] in R

31.1 Ór] þa er or R^2

31.3 svá] ok R^2TUW   óx ... iǫtunn] vǫxtr vindz ok varþ iotunn or U varð] or v. AR^2

31.4–5 Þar ... saman] þær einar ættir koma saman U

31.4–6 Þar ... atalt] om. RA

31.4 Þar] Þar eru R^2 órar] onar T

31.5 kómu] komnar R^2

31.6 því ... atalt] om. U   æ] om. TW   til] eda T; om. W

32.5 baldni] aldni R; balldni A

33.4 fótr] fot A

33.5 gat] om. A

33.6 sexhǫfðaþan] serhǫfðaþann R

34.4 fyrst] fyrst of A

34.5 fremst] frems A   um] of A

35.2 væri iǫrð] iǫrþ veri U   um] om. R^2; of TW

35.4 ec] er TW   um] of AR^{2}TW

35.5 er ... iǫtunn] at froþa iotunn U

35.6 var á] a var AR^{2}UW   um] of R^{2}TW

36.3 oc] e. R

36.5 svá at] sa er A

36.6 æ ... siá] æ maðr um sialfan hann sær A

37.1 heitir] h. iotunn U

37.2 er] hann U

37.4 hans] hann R   vængiom] vængum R^2

37.5 koma] standa U

38.4 um] of A

38.8 varþaþ] varat A

39.5 hann mun] mun hann A

40.2–3 hvar ... dag] om. A

41.1–3 Allir ... dag] om. R

41.1 einheriar] einshæriar A

41.3 hverian] hvern U

42.1 þat] om. A

43.4 um] of A

44.2 freistaþac] fræistaða A

44.3 ec] ec of A

45.1 Lífðrasir] Læifþrasir AR^{2}W; Leidþrasir T; Lifþræser U

45.2 enn ... muno] er þar leynaz meyiar U

45.3 holti Hoddmimis] holldi H. A; Mimis holldi U

45.4–5 morgindǫggvar ... hafa] morgindǫggva þær ok þar U

45.5 sér] er R^2; leynaz T; om. W

45.6 þaðan ... alaz] um alldr alaz U   þaðan] ænn þ. AR^2TW alaz] allar T

46.6 þá] þa þa R

47.3 hana] henni U   fari] fai T

47.4–5 sú ... deyia] su mun renna eða riþa regin U

47.5 þá] om. R^2TW

47.6 módur] modar A; om. U   brautir] braut R^2

49.3 Mǫgþrasis] Mǫgþrasiss R

49.5 þeira] þær er A

51.3 þá] þa þa T   slocnar] sortnar R^2TW

51.4 Móþi] Megi R^2

51.6 oc vinna] Vingnis AR^2TW; Vignigs synir U   vígþroti] vigroþi U

52.5 aldrlagi] aldrelagi R; alldrlagi A

52.6 er] er of A

53.6 vitnis] Vingnis R

54.6 siálfr] ok sialfr A

55.1 manne] manni A

55.5 ec] ec um A

55.6 um] of A

EXPLANATORY NOTES

Title *Vafþrúðnismál* is given this title in red ink in the manuscript. The title is comparable to *Grímnismál*, by which Snorri refers to the poem now known by that name (*Gylfaginning* ch. 21, 36, 40). Snorri never employs a similar title for *Vafþrúðnismál*, though on one occasion, when quoting the poem, Hár observes: *hér segir svá Vafþrúðnir jǫtunn* ("here the giant Vafþrúðnir speaks in this way").

1.2 *mic fara tíðir*: An impersonal construction that may be translated as "I wish to go."

1.6 *við*: In an adversative sense with an understood verb – "to go against" or "to contend against."

2.1 *letia*: Ólsen ("Til Eddakvadene III: Til Vafþrúðnismál"), comparing this passage with *Am.* 48.1–2, argues that *Heima letia* must be translated as "to dissuade (to remain) at home" and thus contradicts *í gǫrðom góða*. He suggests emending *letia* to *hvetia* ("to encourage") and then translates 2.1–3 as "I would eagerly advise High-Father to keep himself at home in the courtyards of the gods." Finnur Jónsson (*De gamle Eddadigte*, 53) also notes that *Heima letia* is a curious expression and speculates that it may be a confusion of two phrases – i.e., "I would wish to detain with dissuasion the High-Father at home." Olsen (*Edda- og skaldekvad*, 11) suggests that the unusualness of the phrase results from Frigg's awareness of Óðinn's resolve to travel, which enables her to express her displeasure with the intended journey by *letia* alone; *letia* would thus be equivalent to "to dissuade from traveling." In 2.3, Olsen suggests, an infinitive phrase meaning "to remain" is understood.

2.2 *munda*: The preterite subjunctive of *munu* is often used with the force of the present.

2.5 *hugða*: Detter and Heinzel (*Sæmundar Edda*, 151) explain that *hyggia* and *vita*, as verbs expressing an ongoing mental state, frequently occur in the preterite when the present might seem required.

4.1 *Heill þú farir*: A common salutation, meaning "good luck," which Finnur Jónsson (*De gamle Eddadigte*, 54) suggests might be taken from the custom of daily life. Cf. *Beowulf* 407: *Wæs þu, Hroðgar, hal!* The phrase can also be used as a valediction, as in *Akv.* 12.7–8: *Heilir farit nú oc horscir, hvars ycr hugr teygir!* ("May you now travel hale and wise, wherever desire leads you").

4.2 *aptr*: In the *Edda*, whenever anaphora is used in the first three lines of *ljóðaháttr*, there are two different sets of alliterating sounds in the two short lines; cf. 3.1–2 and see Salberger ("Heill þú farir!") for further examples. Consequently, Läffler ("Om några underarter," 22–23) suggested emending *aptr* to *fram*, with *Heill* and *heill* then alliterating, as well as *farir* and *fram*. But Salberger points out that there is no paleographic confusion that could have caused the substitution of *aptr* for *fram*, that the logic of the passage suggests that 4.2 should refer to the return journey (4.3 refers to both the outgoing and the return journeys), and that Óðinn especially needs luck to return, not depart. He suggests inserting *af* after *þú* in 4.1.

4.4 *æþi þér dugi*: Either "May (your) mind aid you" or "May (your) mind be strong for you."

4.5 *scalt*: Bugge (*Sæmundar Edda*, 65) suggests that *scalt or* in R is due to scribal anticipation of *orðom*. Interpreting *or* as a form of the personal pronoun *várr* would strain both sense and meter. A similar mistake was made at 7.5, where after *hǫllom* and probably under the suggestion of *órom* the scribe first wrote *or* and then altered it to *frá*.

4.6 *mæla iǫtun*: Though the collocation of *mæla* with an animate object in the accusative case is rare in the *Edda* (Gering, *Die Lieder: Kommentar*, 162), *orðom mæla* occurs in the sense "to speak aggressively" (Ruggerini, "A Stylistic and Typological Approach," 162–65).

5.5 *oc*: The parataxis here is awkward, and so the conjunction might loosely be rendered as "which." See Cleasby and Vigfusson, *An Icelandic-English Dictionary*, s.v., sense A.6, and cf. Noreen, *Altnordische Grammatik*, §473.4.

5.5 *átti*: The alliteration with 5.4 fails. Gering points out that replacing *átti* with *hafði* corrects the flaw but contends that the problem more likely lies with Ímr, a giant about whom little is known (he is not to be confused with Ymir at 21.1 and 28.5). Emending *átti* to *hitti* also restores the alliteration, and a similar usage occurs at *Hrbl.* 53.4: *hittu fǫður Magna* ("you encounter the father of Magni"). Bugge offers the emendation *Hrímnis* ("He Who Brings Frost"), while Finnur Jónsson emends to *Hyms* (cf. *Gylfaginning* ch. 48). Kock suggests that *hǫllo* might be replaced with *inni* ("inn"), but Olsen notes that the word does not occur in the *Edda* (unless here) and that the proximity of *inn* in 5.6 renders it even less likely. Olsen speculates that 5.4 was corrupted in oral transmission and that it originally read *at einni kom [hann] hǫllu*. While a runic inscription from Bergen (B 252) records Ími as the name of a giant associated with both cooking and soot, the simple emendation *Híms* is also a possibility; though etymologically inappropriate, this form may have existed as an aspirated variant that allowed for alliteration. See Gering, *Die Lieder: Kommentar*, 163; Bugge, *Sæmundar Edda*, 65; Finnur Jónsson, *De gamle Eddadigte*, 54; Kock, *Notationes Norroenae*, 17.2202; Olsen, *Edda- og skaldekvad*, 12; Liestøl, "Runer frå Bryggen," 38–40; McKinnell et al., *Runes*, 133; and Noreen, *Altnordische Grammatik*, §306.

6.4–6 *Hitt … iǫtunn*: As Finnur Jónsson points out (*De gamle Eddadigte*, 54), Óðinn here adopts a distinctly superior and confrontational tone. *eþa*, Detter and Heinzel note (*Sæmundar Edda*, 155), is not disjunctive; Óðinn is not so much asking whether Vafþrúðnir is wise or very wise but rather "just how wise are you," and in doing so Óðinn in effect issues a challenge, which the giant quickly accepts.

7.1 *Hvat ... manna*: A "genitive of respect," meaning "who is this man" or, more loosely, "who are you." The phrase may here have a contentious, disrespectful quality, for it is so used elsewhere in the *Edda* in hostile situations (see *Alv.* 2.1 and 5.1, *Bdr.* 5.1, and *Rm.* 1.1).

7.2 *mínom*: The pronoun receives primary stress and alliteration, and so it perhaps reflects Vafþrúðnir's indignation that such a challenger should enter *his* hall of all places.

7.3 *verpomc*: The middle voice of *verpa*, when used with *orð* as the object, means "to speak in a hostile manner." Cf. *Am.* 42.5: *urpuz á orðom* ("They shouted insults," [Dronke, *The Poetic Edda*, 1: 84]). The object of *á* is *er*, and the sense of the phrase is "with whom."

7.4 *comir*: Most editors emend to the indicative *cømr* on the assumption that the intended sense is the future: "you will not come." An optative sense ("may you not come") would also be appropriate, since it would render Vafþrúðnir's observation a charm-like wish and thus be consistent with the confrontational tone of this passage. In Gylfi's entrance to the hall of Hár, Jafnhár, and Þriði (a passage quite possibly modelled on the present one), Snorri uses a subjunctive: *Hann [Gylfi] segir at fyrst vil hann spyrja ef nokkvorr er fróðr maðr inni. Hár segir at hann komi eigi heill út nema hann sé fróðari* ("Gylfi says that first he wishes to learn if any wise man is within. Hár says that he might not come out sound unless he be the wiser" [*Gylfaginning* ch. 2]).

8.1 *Gagnráþr*: This heiti for Óðinn occurs only here and in the list of heiti for Óðinn in Snorri's *Edda* (Faulkes, *Edda*, 66–69); in the latter, the form is Gangráþr, which is what Finnur Jónsson (*De gamle Eddadigte*, 54) prints. The form in R is typically translated as "The One Who Counsels Victory" or "The Victorious One" (so Bugge, *Sæmundar Edda*, 66; Boer, *Die Edda*, 2: 52; Gering, *Die Lieder: Kommentar*, 163). Gangráþr, conversely, would mean "The One Who Counsels Travel" or "The Wanderer," perhaps with the suggestion of "beggar" (Finnur Jónsson, *De gamle Eddadigte*, 54; Olsen, *Edda- og skaldekvad*, 12). Either name, Ejder

("Eddadikten," 11–13) concludes, is appropriate for Óðinn; as the all-powerful god and supervisor of the Valkyries, Óðinn is indeed the god of victories, and as the peripatetic, mysterious prophet, he is equally the god of travelers. A third interpretation is also possible. The first element of Gagnráþr in R may be regarded as the adjectival prefix *gagn-*, meaning "against"; cf. *gagnstöðumaðr*, "adversary," and *gagnsök*, "counter-action" (Cleasby and Vigfusson, *An Icelandic-English Dictionary*, s.v. *gagn-*). The heiti would then mean "The One Who Is Against Counsel" or "The Disputant" and would appropriately characterize Óðinn's role in the poem.

Óðinn's prevarication here stems from two sources. His innate cunning and mystery lead him to conceal his identity lest his adversary, knowing his own defeat to be imminent, should withdraw from the contest; cf. *Baldrs draumar*, where in a situation similar in some ways to *Vafþrúðnismál* Óðinn demands information, and his name is revealed only at the end of the poem. He likewise disguises himself in *Grímnismál* and *Heidreks saga*, while in *Hárbarðzlióð* he claims seldom to reveal his name in the very act of doing so. Also relevant is the primitive belief that an individual's name in and of itself contains power; cf. *Beowulf*, where the hero does not reveal his identity until well after he lands in Denmark. A particularly striking example of this belief occurs in a prose passage early in *Fáfnismál*: *Sigurðr duldi nafns síns, fyr því at þat var trúa þeira í fornescio, at orð feigs mannz mætti mikit, ef hann bölvaði óvin sínom með nafni* ("Sigurðr concealed his name, because in the old heathen time it was believed that the word of one doomed to die had great consequence, if he cursed an enemy by his name"). Finnur Jónsson (*De gamle Eddadigte*, 54) suggests that Óðinn's tone differs here from what it had been in stanza 6. In order to get what he desires (entrance to Vafþrúðnir's hall) Óðinn assumes the posture of a tired, hungry, and almost frightened guest. If slightly less hostile, however, Óðinn is still calculating: in the ritual of entrance, the host must accede to the guest's request, so that Óðinn is here guaranteeing himself entrance further in to the hall and thus moving inexorably towards the wisdom contest.

8.5 *hefi ... farit*: Bugge (*Sæmundar Edda*) punctuates this as a parenthetical clause, so that *þurfi* is parallel with *þyrstr* and predicated upon *emc*, though in this way the syntax becomes convoluted.

9.6 *þulr*: Vafþrúðnir calls himself a *þulr* ("wiseman"), cognate with OE *þyle*, Unferþ's title in *Beowulf* 1165. It is the giant's reputation as a *þulr*, Óðinn tells Frigg in the beginning of *Vafþrúðnismál*, that has attracted the god. The word may have negative connotations, as at *Fm.* 34.2, where the nuthatches refer disparagingly to Regin as *inn hára þul* ("the hoary magician"). If such a sense is operative here, it deepens the irony of the scene: although Vafþrúðnir in effect boasts that he is a crafty wizard, he will nonetheless be defeated by his *gestr*.

10.1 *Óauþigr*: Óðinn furthers the superficially submissive tone of stanza 8. The axiomatic wisdom of 10.1–3 recalls the first part of *Hávamál* in general and stanza 27 in particular: *Ósnotr, er með aldir kømr, / þat er bazt, at hann þegi* ("It is best that a fool who comes among men be silent").

10.1 *maþr*: abbreviated with the M-rune in R.

10.3 occurs verbatim in *Hv.* 19.3 in a catalogue of admonitions; also see *Hv.* 7 and 29.

10.4–5 *ofrmælgi ... geti*: In modern English prose order this would read *ec hygg at ofrmælgi micil geti illa* – "I think that too much boasting has ill results." Cf. *Hv.* 54–56. For the syntax here, cf. *Ls.* 29.4–6: *ørlǫg Frigg hygg ec at ǫll viti* ("I think that Frigg knows all fates").

10.6 *kaldrifiadan*: This adjective, which occurs only here, is an especially appropriate (and graphic) metaphor for a giant who will soon suggest that he and his guest wager their heads. Literally meaning "cold-ribbed," *kaldrifjaðr* has been figuratively interpreted as "malicious" (Finnur Jónsson, *Lexicon Poeticum*, s.v.), "cunning" (Cleasby and Vigfusson, *An Icelandic-English Dictionary*, s.v.), and "hostile" (Neckel, *Edda*, s.v.). Sprenger has argued that this reference to the emotions as situated within the body means that *Vafþrúðnismál* cannot be older than the thirteenth century, but McKinnell has demonstrated that *brjóst* and *hjarta* were used for the seat of the emotions as early as the eleventh century (Sprenger, "*Vafþrúðnismál* 10.3: Der Kaltgerippte," 185–210; McKinnell, "Late Heathen Views," 88 n. 1).

11.3 *um*: *um* and *of* (so A at 22.4 and elsewhere) are untranslatable, preverbal particles that are common in the *Edda* and that are apparently metrically motivated, though the particles do appear in prose, too. The particle lost its originally perfective sense by the beginning of the saga period (cf. the Gothic prefix *ga-* and its development in German), and its placement was gradually delimited to a position before preterite participles. In early texts, *um* and *of* also occur before infinitives, finite verbs, and nouns. The fact that fifteen of the seventeen occurrences in *Vafþrúðnismál* are before infinitives and finite verbs may thus imply an early date for the poem's composition. See Einar Ól. Sveinsson ("Kormakr the Poet," 34 and 42) and, more generally, Jón Helgason (*Tvær kviður fornar*, 180–82) and Fidjestøl, *The Dating of Eddic Poetry*, 207–30.

11.5–6 *er … dróttmǫgo*: Olsen (*Edda- og skaldekvad*, 13) suggests that the series *dregr dag … mǫgo* reflects the scaldic technique of *hendingar* (half and whole rhyme); that is, *dag* and *mǫgo* constitute full rhyme or *aðalhending*, since the stressed vowels *a* and *ǫ* could rhyme in Norse as late as the twelfth century, and all three words are united through half rhyme or *skothending* (consonant rhyme). He posits that Vafþrúðnir acts defiantly by posing as a scald to the lord of the scalds but that Óðinn's own rhetoric is superior when he works a horse reference into each of lines 12.4, 5, and 6 (the Goths were famed for their horses [Finnur Jónsson, *De gamle Eddadigte*, 55]) and plays upon the literal meaning of Scinfaxi with *lýsir* and *mǫn* (12.6).

11.6 *of*: The error of *oc* in R is transparent because of *um dróttmǫgo* which occurs in 12.3.

12.3 *dag*: Snorri recounts the stories of *dagr* and *nótt* in *Gylfaginning* ch. 10.

12.5 *Reiðgotom*: An initial *h* is necessary for alliteration, and the fact that it was lost relatively early in Old Norwegian may be one of the indications of an early date for *Vafþrúðnismál* (see Noreen, *Altnordische Grammatik*, §289). The form with initial *h* occurs on the famous Rǫk stone, and Bugge in fact suggested that the original poet of *Vafþrúðnismál* knew this stone and got the name and other details from it (*Der Runenstein*, 245–48). The Hreiðgoths were apparently eastern Goths, and though the name originally may have meant "nest Goths" or perhaps "Goths of the homeland," the first element evidently came to be understood as merely an epithet meaning "glory" (de Vries, *Altnordisches etymologisches Wörterbuch*, 253); the present form may also merely show folk-etymological association with *reið* ("riding"). The Hreiðgoths are also mentioned in the OE *Elene* 1.20 and in the OE *Widsith* 1.57. See Hill, *Old English Minor Heroic Poems*, 90–91 and references.

13.1–2 *Segdu ... vill*: 13.1–2, 15.1–2, and 17.1–2 are drastically abbreviated in R. Here R reads: *Segdu þ' gagnraþ'*.

13.5 *austan*: As Gering (*Die Lieder: Kommentar*, 166) notes, if the sun and the moon pass from the east to the west, so must the night.

13.6 *of*: *oc* in R is nonsensical and probably arose from the proximity of *nótt*, for the graphs *t* and *c* are similar in R.

13.6 *nýt*: Finnur Jónsson (*De gamle Eddadigte*, 55) points out that such an epithet for the gods is not natural for Vafþrúðnir; it is, rather, the poet's expression.

14.3 *of*: See 13.6 and note.

14.4–6 *méldropa ... dala*: In *Vsp.* 19.5–6 the origin of dew is said to be the world-tree Yggdrasill: *þaðan koma dǫggvar, / þærs í dala falla* ("thence dew comes, that which falls in valleys"). Sigurður Nordal (*Vǫluspá*, 38) observes equivocally that here the poet of *Vǫluspá* "almost appears to have had the stanza from *Vafþrúðnismál* in his mind, though the likeness may have been accidental." Indeed, there is a great likelihood that in alliterative verse *dala* could arise independently in the context of *dǫggvar*.

15.5, 6 *meþ*, *meþ*: The idea here, and also in 16.2, 3, is that the river Ífing constitutes the boundary between the region of the gods and the region of giants (cf. the variant reading in R 16.2, *alda* ["of men,"] corrected in the margin to *iǫtna* ["of giants"]).

16.1 *Ífing*: Since this is the only occurrence of this word, the quantity of the initial *i* is uncertain, as, indeed, is the meaning of the name itself. The derivation is clearer if a long vowel is presumed, but the meaning may be "Yew River" as easily as "The Violent One," the sense recorded in the Index of Names (de Vries, *Altnordisches etymologisches Wörterbuch*, 283–84; Olsen, *Edda- og skaldekvad*, 14). The river that is free of ice and ever-flowing is an archetypal symbol of life.

16.1 *á*: Here and at 18.1, Óðinn's answer repeats the species (river, horse) of what he is describing, but it does not at 12.1 and 14.1 (Boer [*Die Edda*, 2: 52] compares *Grm.* 22, 25, and 26). This kind of variation is characteristic of oral poetics.

16.4 *opin*: In an adverbial sense – free from ice.

16.6 *verþrat*: The enclitic -*at*, which can be qualitatively altered by a preceding vowel, is a common verbal negation in the *Edda*.

17.5 *finnaz*: A true middle voice meaning "(they) will find each other," though the phrase is a common way of saying "they will meet."

17.6 *Surtr*: Sigurður Nordal (*Vǫluspá*, 102) notes that Surtr "was thought of as a mighty giant in the underworld who had an especial power over fire. He is therefore unlike all other giants in his nature, as they are the rulers of frost and cold" (cf. *Vaf.* 21.5 and 50.6). His connection with fire seems to have made Surtr of particular interest to the Icelanders, who of course knew of the power of fire through the volcanoes.

17.6 *sváso*: As with *nýt* (13.6), this epithet is more natural from the poet than from Vafþrúðnir.

18 *Óðinn qvaþ*: Beginning with this stanza, the abbreviations *o.q.* and *v.q.* accompany the dialogue in the margin of R. Similar attributions are marginally (and extrametrically) added in *For Scírnis*, *Hárbarðzlióð*, and *Locasenna*. This stanza is quoted and its ideas expanded upon in *Gylfaginning* ch. 51.

18.1 *Vígriþr*: The same place is perhaps intended by *Óscopnir* ("The Misshapen One") in *Fm.* 15.1.

18.4 *rasta*: A "partitive genitive," often used with cardinal numbers. A *rǫst* was the distance between two resting places on a journey, and consequently its absolute distance varied in accordance with the journey; five or six miles is a convenient estimate. *hundraþ rasta* may have been a conventional way to imply a great distance, for in *Gylfaginning* ch. 27 it is also the distance which Heimdallr is able to see *frá sér* ("from himself").

18.5 *hverian veg*: That is, in each direction.

18.6 *sá ... vitaþr*: "that is the valley known to them," or more idiomatically "that is the valley they know." It is also possible that the sense of *vitaþr* here is "determined," "foreseen," for these senses are recorded for *vita*, though the latter only when in conjunction with *fram* or *fyrir* (Finnur Jónsson, *Lexicon Poeticum*, s.v. *vita* senses 6–7). Preterite participles in compound verbs may be inflected in the neuter or, as here, to show concord with the subject.

19.4 *Hǫfði veðia*: It may be recalled here that Óðinn already possesses the head of Mimir, which *sagði ... honum mǫrg tíðendi ór ǫðrum heimum* ("said to him many things from other worlds," *Ynglinga saga* ch. 7). The head likewise serves as a synecdoche for life in the *Hǫfuðlausn* ("head-ransom") poems that both Egill Skallagrímsson and Óttarr svarti compose to save their lives.

19.6 *geðspeki*: There seems to be little if any difference between *geðspeki* and *fornom stǫfom* (1.5), at least as they are displayed in this poem. *geðspeki* occurs about two thirds of the way into a line in R; *capitulum* is written in red in the remaining space.

20 These stanzas treat the same material as *Gylfaginning* ch. 10–11.

20.1–3 *Segðu ... vitir*: The semantic distinction between 20.2 and 20.3 is inconsequential, and the phrases seem to have been joined only as a metrical formula. Cf. 22.1–3 and *Rm.* 19.1–3: *Segðu mér þat, Hnicarr, / allz þú hvárttveggia veizt, / goða heill oc guma* ("Tell me that, Hnicarr, since you know the omens of both the gods and men").

20.2 *œþi*: A begins with this word at the top of a folio. Marginal *o.q.* and *v.q.*, to identify the speakers, occur in A as well as in R.

20.6 *inn*: The definite article often precedes a vocative.

21 Cf. *Grm.* 40–41 and *Gylfaginning* ch. 7–8. The verbal similarities with *Grm.* 40 are particularly striking: *Ór Ymis holdi var iǫrð um scǫpuð, / enn ór sveita sær, / biǫrg ór beinom / baðmr ór hári / enn ór hausi himinn* ("From the body of Ymir the earth was created but the seas from his blood, the mountains from his bones, a tree from his hair, and the sky from his skull"). Gering (*Die Lieder: Kommentar*, 167) implies that stanza 21 in *Vafþrúðnismál* is a rearrangement of the more detailed version in *Grímnismál*, though clear lines of influence in Eddic poetry are extremely difficult to identify.

21.3 *en*: As a connective, *en* has a slightly adversative sense in comparison with *oc* and is typically used to join unrelated but not necessarily contrary statements. Cf. the use of *oc* in 23.3.

21.6 *sveita*: Though literally *sveiti* means "sweat," it is often used metaphorically for blood (e.g. *Fm.* 32.2); in the corresponding passage in *Gylfaginning* Snorri in fact uses *blóð*.

22 Henceforth in both R and A the formulaic beginning of Óðinn's stanzas is drastically abbreviated. Here, for example, R actually reads *Segðu þ' ii e. þ. ę. d.*

22.5 *svá at*: *sá ær* in A mirrors *sá er* at 24.5, though the form in R is equally acceptable here. Cf. 36.5.

23.1 *Mundilfœri*: *Vsp.* 5–6 explain how the sun and the moon got their names and positions in the sky, and *Grm.* 37 and 39 respectively discuss the horses that pull the sun's chariot and the wolves that pursue them. Finnur Jónsson (*Lexicon Poeticum*, s.v.) interprets the name as Mundilfari, which he translates as "the one who moves himself according to fixed times."

23.5 *hverian dag*: An "accusative of time" meaning "each day."

23.6 *ǫldom at ártali*: "According to time-reckoning among men." Cf. *Vsp.* 6.10, *árom at telia* ("to count by years"), and see *Alv.* 14.6, where we are told that the elves call the moon *ártali*. The scribe of A originally wrote *alldtali* but then added *ar* above *alld*.

24.2 *allz ... qveþa*: The formulaic variation of *ef þitt œþi dugir, allz þic svinnan qveþa*, and *allz þic fróþan qveþa* is constrained by alliteration; i.e. *annat* and *œþi* alliterate in 22.1–2, but *Segðu* and *svinnan* here and *fiórða* and *fróþan* in 26.1–2. Though 24.2–3 may simply be formulaic, and so without any special significance for this passage in particular, the distinction between the indicative of *qveða* and the subjunctive mood of *vitir* might imply a potential discrepancy between what is said about Vafþrúðnir's wisdom and how wise he actually is. The subjunctive would then indicate that Vafþrúðnir has yet to prove his wisdom to Óðinn and possibly that Óðinn, knowing the giant not to be as wise as he is reputed to be, here provokes him.

25.2, 3 *dags, nótt*: Most editors capitalize these forms as personifications, but given the cosmological nature of the passage they seem to refer simply to *dagr* and *nótt*, just as the references at 23.2 and 23.3 refer simply to the moon and sun respectively.

25.3 *Nǫrvi*: Nǫrr is also mentioned as the father of *nótt* in *Alv.* 29.

26.1–3 Cf. *Fm.* 12.1–3: *Segðu mér, Fáfnir, / allz þik fróðan qveða / oc vel mart vita.*

27.1 *Vindsvalr*: In *Gylfaginning* ch. 19 Snorri equates Vindsvalr with Vindlóni; the father, Snorri explains, was Vásuðr, and the whole family was fierce and cold-hearted.

27.2, 3 *vetrar, sumars*: Editors often treat these as personifications. See 25.2 and 3, and note.

27.3 *Svásuþr*: This is generally translated as "The Beloved One" or "The Merciful One" and is derived, presumably, from the adjective *sváss* ("beloved") and the abstract suffix *-uðr / -unnr*. The word should then be feminine (see Noreen, *Altnordische Grammatik*, §384.2), though it presumably was interpreted as a masculine personification. The value judgment implied by "beloved," however, seems inconsistent with the functional way in which the cosmos is described throughout this passage; the father of the sun, for instance, is "The Shining One" and the father of winter "The Wind-Cool One." *sváss* is etymologically a possessive pronoun (cognate with Lat *suus*; cf. OE *swæs* for a similar development) meaning "one's own," and though this sense seems absent in Norse, there are passages that suggest a sense less subjective than "beloved." In *Akv.* 1.8, *sváss* modifies *bjór* and is translated by Dronke (*The Poetic Edda*, 1: 3) as "delicious," and Cleasby and Vigfusson (*An Icelandic-English Dictionary*) cite a passage in the *Grágás* (the Icelandic laws) where the negative *úsváss* modifies *veðr*. *-suþr* suggests *suþr* ("south"), and so in keeping with the other lineages in this passage the meaning of *Svásuþr* may well be "The Mild South," a reference to the direction from which summer enters Scandinavia. Auden and Taylor (*Norse Poems*, 230) translate as simply "South." The medial consonants in *Svássuþr* could be expected to reduce to -ss- (Noreen, *Altnordische Grammatik*, §285).

27.3 *sumars*: The stanza is obviously truncated. Bugge (*Sæmundar Edda*, 69) records the following completion in many paper manuscripts: *ár of bæði þau / skulu ey fara / unz rjúfask regin* ("Forever those both must travel until the gods are destroyed"). This completion may well have been modeled on 52.6 or on *Ls.* 41.3, where *unz riufaz regin* in fact occurs. The absence of the final half-stanza in both R and A indicates it was not present in the common archetype of these manuscripts, and the continuation in the paper manuscripts may well be a late attempt to correct a text that was damaged very early in its transmission. Bugge postulates a continuation from the corresponding passage in *Gylfaginning* (see note to 27.1), but this reconstruction is necessarily speculative: *Vindsvals faðir / var Vásuðr of heitinn / öll er sú ætt til ötul* ("Vindsvalr's father was called Vásuðr; the entire lineage is very fierce"). Neckel (*Edda*, 49) notes a different reconstruction from Snorri by Wimmer: *var Vindsvalr / Vásuði borinn, / ǫll er sú kaldrifiuð kin* ("Vindsvalr was born to Vásuðr, the entire race is 'cold-ribbed'").

28.4–6 *hverr ... árdaga*: Bugge (*Sæmundar Edda*, 69) points out that Vafþrúðnir seems to answer only the last part of the question (about the giants) and so he suggests emending *ása* to *iǫtna*, which Sijmons in fact prints; *eþa* is difficult here, but since at 34.5 it connects two almost identical statements (and cf. 6.6), Gering (*Die Lieder*: Kommentar, 170) suggests that *iǫtna* has "the greatest probability." The passage is still confusing, however, for logically the eldest *Ymis niðia* ought to be Ymir himself, though Vafþrúðnir implies it is Aurgelmir (29.6) who is oldest; even if Ymir and Aurgelmir are one and the same (see note to 29.6), Óðinn in effect answers his own question as he asks it. As the passage stands, it may be best to interpret it as asking disjunctively from which race the oldest being came: "Who, whether from the gods or the giants, is the oldest?"

29.1–2 *ørófi ... scǫpuþ*: The subjunctive *væri* is used because at the time being discussed the earth had not been created and was only a possibility. The dative *ørófi* may derive from what is in effect the comparative sense of *áþr* (Gering, *Die Lieder: Kommentar*, 170), though the two phrases have the appearance of a formula (cf. 35.1–2), which, like an idiom, often defies precise grammatical explanation. The dative singular of the adjective *langr*, *lǫngu*, is often similarly used to mean "long since."

29.3 *Bergelmir*: The first element of the name has been variously derived from *berg* ("mountain," Bugge, *Sæmundar Edda*, 69; Boer, *Die Edda*, 2: 54) and from *ber* ("bear," Finnur Jónsson, *De gamle Eddadigte*, 57; de Vries, *Altnordisches etymologisches Wörterbuch*, 33). *berg* is perhaps the more likely root, for as Kock ("Ordforskning i den äldre Eddan," 137) points out, giants often live in rocks and the root *berg* certainly figures in other compounds (e.g. *bergbúi* ["rock-dweller"] and *berghlíð* ["the side of a rocky hill"], Cleasby and Vigfusson, *An Icelandic-English Dictionary*, s.v.). But since the name occurs only a few times in Norse literature (here, at 35.3, *Gylfaginning* ch. 7, where stanza 35 is quoted, and among the heiti of giants in Snorri's *Edda* [Faulkes, *Edda*, 156]), a definitive etymology is doubtful. Boer suggests that Þrúdgelmir and Aurgelmir are back-formations of Bergelmir, and in any event the recurrence of the element *-gelmir* identifies the three as members of one family. Olsen (*Edda- og skaldekvad*, 15), who cites several river names that contain the element *-gelmir* and who interprets the root of Bergelmir as *berg*, contends that this stanza embodies an origin myth relating how in primitive times the giants built a great river course. See Introduction, pp. 32–34, for Boer's suggested rearrangement of the following stanzas.

29.6 *Aurgelmir*: In *Gylfaginning* ch. 5 Snorri states that Aurgelmir is the name by which the *hrímþursar* know Ymir, a connection also made in stanzas 30 and 31, which may have been Snorri's source.

30.4–6 *hvaþan ... iǫtunn*: 30.4–6 and all of stanza 31 are quoted in *Gylfa-ginning* ch. 5. As a result of the way Snorri incorporates these lines, 30.6 refers to Aurgelmir, while in *Vafþrúðnismál* it clearly is a vocative addressing Vafþrúðnir, as it is also at 20.6.

31.1 *Élivágom*: In *Gylfaginning* ch. 5 Snorri relates in detail how the rivers formed into poisonous drops that in turn fell into Ginnungagap and were then transformed into Ymir.

31.3 *svá óx unz*: "it grew thus until."

31.4–6 *þar ... atalt*: These lines survive only in the manuscripts of *Gyl-faginning*; the text printed here is taken from R² and T. Though the *Edda* manuscripts contain a good deal of variation (see Textual Notes), there is no reason to doubt the authenticity of the lines. Bugge (*Sæmundar Edda*, 70) records that many paper manuscripts read instead: *en síum fleigði / ór suðheimi / hyrr gaf hrími fjör* ("it cast seas from the southern region, fire gave life to the frost"). This variant seems to derive from *Gylfaginning* ch. 5.

31.6 *því ... atalt*: *því* here functions as a conjunction meaning "therefore." *þat*, the subject of the clause, evidently refers to *órar ættir* in 31.4, since as Faulkes (*Gylfaginning*, 159) notes, "In some cases *þat* is in the nature of an indefinite subject, or refers to a whole phrase or concept rather than to a specific noun." Gering (*Die Lieder: Kommentar*, 171) compares this passage with *Hv.* 49.4, where *þat* refers to *tveim trémǫnnum* ("two scarecrows"), and suggests the meaning is "for that reason, the whole giant race is always too fierce."

32.5 *baldni iǫtunn*: Ymir/Aurgelmir might equally be called "old," as in R, but the alliterative pattern requires a *b* and thereby suggests that *aldni* is simply a scribal error.

32.6 *hafdit*: Here the negative enclitic *-at* assimilates with the final *-i* of *hafði*. Cf. 16.6 and note.

33 In *Gylfaginning* ch. 5 Snorri recounts this episode as follows: *Þá óx undir vinstri hǫnd honum maðr ok kona, ok annarr fótr hans gat son við ǫðrum* ("Then a man and a woman grew under his left arm, and one foot begot a son with the other"). Gering (*Die Lieder: Kommentar*, 171) suggests that 33.3 refers to a male *and* a female, not a hermaphrodite, though *saman* would seem to render the latter interpretation possible.

33.5 *ins fróða iǫtuns*: Grammatically this phrase could modify either *fótr* or *son*, though the latter is syntactically the more likely alternative.

33.6 *sexhǫfðaþan*: Multi-headed giants occur elsewhere in the *Edda* (see *Skm.* 31 and *Hym.* 8 and 35). In each of these cases (and so presumably here) the mutation seems intended to suggest hideousness.

34.2 *fróþan*: As they stand in R and A, 34.1 and 34.2 lack alliteration. Bugge (*Sæmundar Edda*, 70) suggests that the alliteration might involve *átta* and *allz*, but Gering (*Die Lieder: Kommentar*, 172) regards such alliteration as doubtful. The simplest emendation and the one adopted by most editors is to substitute *svinnan* for *fróþan*; cf. 36.2 and 30.2, where A reads *fróþan*, which does not alliterate, and R reads *svinnan*, which does. For a thorough discussion see Salberger ("Ett stavrims-problem").

34.4–5 *hvat ... veitzt*: There is apparently no semantic distinction between 34.4 and 34.5 (cf. note to 20.2–3); alliterative stress falls on the adverbs *fyrst* and *fremst* and thus underscores Óðinn's central concern in the question.

35 This stanza is quoted in *Gylfaginning* ch. 7.

35.6 *lúðr*: A notoriously difficult word with an obscure etymology (de Vries, *Altnordisches etymologisches Wörterbuch*, 367), *lúðr* has been defined as "cradle," "bier," "boat," "mill," and "trumpet." In *Gylfaginning* ch. 7, Snorri precedes this stanza with a discussion that treats Bergelmir as a Norse Noah and implies that a *lúðr* is an ark: *Synir Bors drápu Ymi jǫtun.*

En er hann fell, þá hljóp svá mikit blóð ór sárum hans at með því drektu þeir allri ætt hrímþursa, nema einn komsk undan með sínu hýski. Þann kalla jǫtnar Bergelmi. Hann fór upp á lúðr sinn ok kona hans ok helzk þar, ok eru af þeim komnar hrímþursar ættir ... ("The sons of Borr killed the giant Ymir. And when he died so much blood poured out of his wounds that it drowned the entire race of giants; only one escaped with his family. The giants call him Bergelmir. He and his wife went up on to his *lúðr* and kept themselves there, and from them descend the race of frost-giants"). Such a meaning for *lúðr* is forced, at least for *Vafþrúðnismál*, for as Turville-Petre ("Professor Dumézil," 212) points out, "the poem, as we understand it, provides no basis for Snorri's story of the flood. Therefore, we have no evidence of a flood in Norse myth, but Snorri, who knew the story of Noah, felt the need of one" (also see Turville-Petre, *Myth and Religion*, 276). Christiansen ("Det norrøne ord lúðr") argues that Bergelmir must be older than Vafþrúðnir, so that the latter would need to remember the former's death, not birth, and Detter and Heinzel (*Sæmundar Edda*, 163) and Holtsmark ("Det norrøne ord lúðr") also interpret *lúðr* as "bier." Olsen (*Edda- og skaldekvad*, 17) stresses the importance of the preposition *á* ("on"), rather than *í* ("in"), and the long progeny implied in stanza 31 to argue that Bergelmir lived a long life and consequently that *lúðr* cannot mean "cradle" but instead must mean "hand-mill" – presumably a symbol of his fertility. The argument that Vafþrúðnir must be younger than Bergelmir is perhaps overly literal, and whatever the differences between *á* and *í*, stanza 31 refers to Aurgelmir, not Bergelmir. Either "cradle" or "bier" is thematically acceptable, though one might argue that in answer to a question about an earliest memory, recollection of a beginning, suggested by a birth, is more thematically and stylistically appropriate, and so "cradle" is the meaning recorded in the Glossary. Óðinn evidently asks this question of Vafþrúðnir because of the giant's great age; see 9.6, where Vafþrúðnir refers to himself as *gamli*.

36.3 *oc*: As with all of Óðinn's questions in this section, the first three lines are abbreviated in R and A. The former reads *Segðu þ' iþ ix. a. þ. s. q. e.*, but the latter's abbreviation breaks off after 36.2. The *e* in R has been expanded as both *ef* (Hildebrand, *Die Lieder*; Boer, *Die Edda*) and *eða* (Neckel, *Edda*), and also emended to *oc* (Bugge, *Sæmundar Edda*; Sijmons, *Die Lieder: Text*; Jón Helgason, *Eddadigte: Gudedigte*). Given the structure of Óðinn's other questions, the second alternative seems the most likely; the scribe may have accidentally written *e*, standing for *eþa*, under the influence of *qveþa* in 36.2.

36.6 *æ ... siá*: That is, men never see the wind itself. The meaning of "never" for *æ* is recorded by both Finnur Jónsson (*Lexicon Poeticum*, s.v.) and Neckel (*Edda*, s.v.), but the present passage is the only instance cited, though there is an example in Fritzner's Norwegian Homily Book. For a similar, rarely used negative see *ey* at 55.1. The confused reading of A (see Textual Notes) is doubtless due to the peculiar usage here of *æ*. Emendation to *æva* ("never") would improve the sense, but the large number of initial unstressed syllables would then make the line metrically suspect. Reichardt ("A Contribution," 203) suggests emending to *æ maðr hann siálfan né sér* ("a man does not always see himself"), but such a reading would make little sense in context. For Snorri's version of this passage see *Gylfaginning* ch. 18, where he quotes stanza 37.

37.1 *Hræsvelgr*: Martin ("Ár vas alda," 359) speculates that the "reference to a corpse-devouring eagle in *Voluspá* 50 and *Skírnismál* [*Skm.*] 27 may be an allusion to Hræsvelgr." The latter passage does not actually describe the eagle devouring corpses, but such scavenging might be considered implicit in any reference to the bird.

38.2 *tíva rǫc*: The Ragnarǫk itself may not be intended here but simply the history of the gods. *tíva*, in place of *ragna*, sustains the alliteration. Rather than continuing to address Vafþrúðnir as simply *svinnr* or *fróðr*, Óðinn begins to refer to the giant's knowledge of *tíva rǫc ǫll* when the nature of the questions turns from cosmogonical to eschatological. The alteration is in a sense the poet's rather than Óðinn's, for Óðinn does not in fact ask about the Ragnarǫk, though it does figure in Vafþrúðnir's answer. The subjunctive *vitir* (38.3) may again be interpreted as a reflection of Óðinn's doubt about the extent of Vafþrúðnir's knowledge.

38.4 *Niǫrðr*: Niǫrðr follows from stanzas 36 and 37, for he is the keeper of the winds (*Gylfaginning* ch. 23).

38.5 *meþ ása sonom*: The alliteration again breaks down. Suggested emendations include *Nóatúnom*, *til Nóatúna*, *ór Nóatúnom* (Nóatún is the home of Niǫrðr in *Grm.* 16), and *með niðjum ása*. The latter, printed by Finnur Jónsson (*De gamle Eddadigte*), is attractive and has been widely accepted. It is very doubtful whether the preverbal particle *um* and *ása* can alliterate, as has also been suggested, and indeed in similar constructions in 20.4–5, 22.4–5, 24.4–5, and 26.4–5 it is the subject of the clause that alliterates. The problems with this stanza go beyond 38.5, however, for as Gering (*Die Lieder: Kommentar*, 173) observes, 38.6–7 are "without doubt interpolated": the idea is not well-integrated, and the double alliteration of 38.6 and the end-rhyme of *-om* in 38.5, 6, and 7 are suspicious. *ásom* in 38.8, if it is original, would suggest that *ása* in 38.5 is indeed a substitution or an interpolation: the poet would not have been likely to use the same word in adjoining lines (assuming 38.6–7 are late additions).

38.6 *hofom*: Foote and Wilson (*The Viking Achievement*, 398) observe, "In twelfth- and thirteenth-century sources the word *hof* is regularly used for 'heathen temple' (apparently thought of as similar to a church) and this decisive linking of the word with pagan cult-places cannot be entirely without foundation. The most recent study of temples in heathen Scandinavia concludes, however, that the name is to be taken to mean not a special building containing images of the gods and exclusively reserved for cult gatherings, but rather a farmstead at which it was the custom to foregather for cult celebrations, chiefly doubtless for the regular seasonal feasts." (See further Olaf Olsen, *Hørg, Hov og*

Kirke.) Even if *hof* here retains its etymological meaning of "hall" or "household," it is often linked with *hǫrgr* in a context that implies a connection with worship (see Cleasby and Vigfusson, *An Icelandic-English Dictionary*, s.v., and Sigurður Nordal, *Vǫluspá*, 21).

38.8 *oc ... alinn*: "and he was not born among the gods."

39.2 *scópo*: An odd verb here; in *Gylfaginning* ch. 23 Snorri implies nothing out of the ordinary about Niǫrðr's birth and maturation: *Hann var upp fæddr í Vanaheimum* ("He was raised in Vanaheim").

39.2 *vís*: For an evaluative adjective similarly inappropriate for Vafþrúðnir, see 13.6 and 17.6. *víss* is often formulaically combined with *Vanir* in the *Edda* (e.g. *Skm.* 17.3 and 18.3, and *Sd.* 18.7), while *regin* is typically reserved for the *Æsir*. *regin* may be used here to recall the Ragnarǫk and thus further the transition to the remainder of the poem.

39.3 *gíslingo*: After the ancient battle between the Æsir and the Vanir, who are characterized by prescience and fertility, the Vanir gave Niǫrðr and Freyr as hostages to the Æsir as part of the settlement. See *Gylfaginning* ch. 23 and *Ynglinga saga* ch. 4. See further de Vries (*Altgermanische Religionsgeschichte*, 474–75), Turville-Petre (*Myth and Religion*, 156–62), and Dumézil (*Gods of the Ancient Northmen*, 3–25).

39.4 *aldar rǫc*: Still another variation on Ragnarǫk, again predicated upon alliteration (*aldar ... aptr*).

39.5–6 *hann ... vǫnom*: This return is not mentioned in the account in *Ynglinga saga*. The idea seems to be that as a consequence (or perhaps sign) of the Ragnarǫk, fertility, represented by the Vanir in general and Niǫrðr in particular, will depart from the world.

40 This stanza is obviously damaged, and Bugge (*Sæmundar Edda*) and Finnur Jónsson (*De gamle Eddadigte*) print 41.4–6 both where it is and as 40.4–6, but it is very unlikely and without corroboration in *Vafþrúðnismál* that three entire lines in the question and answer would be identical; even 14.1–3, 16.1–3, and 18.1–3 show some variation from

the questions they answer. Sijmons (*Die Lieder: Text*) prints the lines as follows: *Segþu þat et ellifta, / alz þik svinnan kveþa, / ok þú, Vafþrúþner, viter: / hvar ýtar túnom í ... hǫggvask hverjan dag?* Hildebrand (*Die Lieder*) offers a similar reconstruction, wherein 4–5 read: *hverir'u ýtar / es í Óþins túnum.* Yet another possibility would be a stanza that began like 38.1–3 and continued *hvar ýta synir / Óþins túnom í / hǫggvask hverian dag.* Originally, in any case, lines 1–3 of stanza 40 must certainly have followed the pattern of the other stanzas in this passage, so that 40.2–3 might well be derived from a lost 40.4–6. But the variation between these lines in R and A suggests more strongly that their archetype, for whatever reason, had only what is here printed as 40.1 and that 40.2–3 are an attempt by the scribe of R to reconstruct the absent question from its answer in stanza 41. It should first be noted that A has only abbreviations for 40.1 and then all of stanza 41 as it is printed here, so that it offers no clues about the nature or existence of the archetype after 40.1. But in none of his responses to Óðinn's eleven other numbered questions does Vafþrúðnir repeat the final line of the question in the third line of the answer, so the recurrence of 40.3 at 41.3 is suspicious. Moreover, although *ýtar* does occur in skaldic verse, it is a relatively rare word in Eddic poetry, occurring only here and in variations on the phrase *synir ýta* at *Hv.* 28.5, 68.2, 147.3, and 164.3. Its rarity may well imply that it was specifically picked to alliterate with *ellipta*, and, in light of Sijmon's plausible reconstruction, *ýtar* would so alliterate only in a damaged stanza wherein it was the second line rather than the fourth. In other words, the scribe of A quite possibly recorded exactly what was in the archetype, while the scribe of R, in an attempt to construct a question and an answer from a damaged exemplar, drew 40.3 from 41.3 and created 40.2 on the implications of 41.1–2. He then omitted 41.1–3 because of eyeskip from 40.3 to 41.3 or because he wished to avoid repeating material he had just used in fashioning the question. The repetition of *q.* and *v.* is inconclusive one way or the other; the marginal placement of the attributions in both R and A implies that they were so placed in the archetype, and accordingly they would not (and do not in R and A) precisely indicate where within the line of text stanza 40 ended and stanza 41 began. The formulaic language of *Vafþrúðnismál* and the abbreviations used to represent it would certainly have been conducive to the sort of scribal error postulated. The reading of R for stanza 40 is here preserved in accordance with the objective of maintaining the integrity of this manuscript; the authenticity of 41.1–3 is suggested by A, by the manuscripts of *Gylfaginning* (ch. 41, where stanza 41 is quoted as it appears in A), and by the fact that these lines are necessary for the sense of the passage. Bugge (*Sæmundar Edda*, 71) records the following reading from the paper manuscripts: *Segðu þat et ellipta / alls þú tíva rök / öll, Vafþrúðnir, vitir / hvat einherjar vinna / Herjaföðrs at, / unz rjúfask regin* ("Tell that eleventh, Vafþrúðnir, since you might know all the fates of the gods: what do the champions of Óðinn do until the gods are destroyed").

41.1 *einheriar*: Óðinn's champions are called the "only champions" both because in the afterlife they are the only warriors and because they are so great that in comparison no one else deserves the title champion. For other accounts of them and their activities, see *Eiríksmál*, *Grímnismál* 18–19, and *Gylfaginning* ch. 38–41. Ólsen ("Til Eddakvadene II: Til Hávamál," 73) accepts *einshæriar* of A and translates as "all those who belong to one and the same host," but as Gering (*Die Lieder: Kommentar*, 174) notes, the reading of *Gylfaginning* ch. 41, where this stanza is quoted, is supported by *Grm.* 18.6, 23.4, 36.9, and 51.5, and by *HHI* 38.5.

41.4 *val ... kiósa*: This refers not to the Valkyries but to the fact that they kill each other. The collocation *val ... kiósa*, however, would almost certainly have evoked the image of the Valkyries for a medieval audience, and so the masculine pronoun *þeir* may have been particularly jarring.

41.5–6 *oc ... saman*: Bugge (*Sæmundar Edda*, 72) notes the following substitution in the paper manuscripts: *öl með ásum drekka / ok seðjask Sæhrímni* ("they drink ale with the gods and satisfy themselves with the boar Sæhrimnir").

41.6 *sitia ... saman*: "thereafter [*meirr*] they sit together at peace." With this usage of *meirr* cf. *Rþ.* 37.1–2: *Reið hann meirr þaðan / myrcan við* ("Thereafter he rode thence through the dark forest").

42 Gering (*Die Lieder: Kommentar*, 174) notes, "Before Óðinn begins his second series of questions, he inquires where Vafþrúðnir might have acquired his great knowledge."

42.2 *hví*: Finnur Jónsson (*De gamle Eddadigte*, 59) translates as "how" and notes that though *hvé* would be expected, *hví* can be used with this meaning. Consequently, he prints 42.6 as *þú hit sannasta segir*, the natural order for an indirect question, and places a full-stop after *segir*. Though this reading is possible, such a use for *hví* is strained, and it may be better to translate *hví* as simply "why." The lines 42.4–7 thus contain Óðinn's concession that Vafþrúðnir does in fact know many things, and 42.1–3 ask through an indirect question why this is the case.

43.4 *heim*: In *Vsp.* 2.5 the Sybil observes *nío man ec heima* ("I remember nine worlds"). Finnur Jónsson (*De gamle Eddadigte*, 60) regards 43.4 as "without any doubt inauthentic," because it says essentially the same thing as 43.5. But in conjunction with 43.5, 43.4 may be regarded as Vafþrúðnir's way of stressing the significance of what he has done; i.e. the giant traveled through *each* world, *and* there were *nine* in all. Bugge (*Sæmundar Edda*), Boer (*Die Edda*), Gering (*Die Lieder: Kommentar*), Finnur Jónsson (*De gamle Eddadigte*), and Neckel (*Edda*) print this line as two separate half-lines with the caesura after *ec*; Hildebrand (*Die Lieder*) and Jón Helgason (*Eddadigte: Gudedigte*) print the line as here. While the line does have more unstressed syllables than is customary in a Full Line in *ljóðaháttr*, the syntax does not suggest that there is a caesura after *ec* (cf. 38.4, where there clearly is a caesura). *hvern, heim,* and *komit* may be regarded as the three lifts, and *hefi* as an unaccented word (which is often the case with verbs) with incidental alliteration.

43.4 *komit*: *koma* with an accusative object in the sense "to travel through" (or "into") is extremely rare; for the more frequent usage of *koma* with a dative, see Cleasby and Vigfusson, *An Icelandic-English Dictionary,* s.v., sense B. Cf. *Am.* 10.1–2: *Sæing fóro síðan / sína þau Hǫgni* ("Afterwards those two, Hǫgni and his wife, went to their bed").

43.5–7 *nío ... halir: fyr neðan* almost always means "beneath" (Cleasby and Vigfusson, *An Icelandic-English Dictionary,* s.v. *neðan*; cf. Gering, *Die Lieder: Kommentar,* 174), and so these nine regions are apparently not the same as the nine regions mentioned in *Vsp.* 2.5: i.e. Ásgarðr, Miðgarðr, etc. (see further Nordal, *Vǫluspá,* 9, and Faulkes, *Edda: Prologue and Gylfaginning,* 106; Finnur Jónsson, *Lexicon Poeticum,* s.v. *neðan,* regards the reference as collective and translates the phrase as "down in the under-world"). *Vsp.* 2.6 mentions *nío íviðiur* ("nine ogresses") as a part of the Sybil's memory, and these nine are perhaps collectively the god Heimdallr's mother. In any event, *Vsp.* 2.5–6, like the present stanza, associates giants with nine worlds. If *helio* in 43.7 is presumed to be a place, the meaning of these lines becomes difficult, for the distinction between Hel and Niflhel is unclear (Gering, *Die Lieder: Kommentar,* 174). Thus, both Gering and Finnur Jónsson (*De gamle Eddadigte,* 60) suggest that *ór helio* is a later scribal addition, and Gering also indicates that *hinig of deyia halir* might be the correct reading, although lines metrically similar to that in R occur elsewhere in the poem (cf. 41.6). But if *helio* is here understood as simply "death," the passage becomes much clearer. This meaning is most common outside Eddic poetry (Cleasby and Vigfusson, *An Icelandic-English Dictionary,* s.v. *hel* sense 2), but it also occurs in *Am.* 97.7–8: *hálft gecc til heliar / ór húsi þíno* ("half of your household went to their deaths"). Cf. Dronke, *The Poetic Edda* 1: 96 and see further Ellis

Davidson, *The Road to Hel*, 83–87. The image would then be that warriors (*halir*) die in some way successively through nine regions beneath Niflhel. Perhaps under the influence of *Vsp.* 39, which describes a region of the dead inhabited by oath-breakers and murderers and which itself may have been indirectly influenced by Revelations 21.8, when Snorri approached this passage he reworked it in more familiar, Christian terms. In *Gylfaginning* ch. 3 he evidently understands Niflhel as the ninth world and utilizes the moral condition of individuals to explain why they should pass through the several worlds: *vándir menn fara til Heljar ok þaðan í Niflhel, þat er niðr í inn níunda heim* ("wicked men travel to Hel and thence to Niflhel, that is, down into the ninth world"). (It was presumably because of Snorri's version that Finnur Jónsson [*De gamle Eddadigte*, 60] suggests *fyr neðan* means "down.") The inauthenticity of Snorri's moral interpretation is further revealed at *Gylfaginning* ch. 34, where he contradicts his earlier criterion for entrance to Niflhel by saying that *sóttdauðir menn ok ellidauðir* ("men who die from sickness and old age") reside in it.

44 Óðinn begins the final series of questions, which is structurally emphasized by the alteration in the question formula. The implication of these lines, Finnur Jónsson (*Den oldnorske*, 140) suggests, is "but never have I encountered one like you." It is the information on the Ragnarǫk about which Óðinn has presumably been most curious all along, and so the switch from indirect to direct questioning perhaps reflects greater interest and intensity on Óðinn's part. The remaining stanzas correspond to *Gylfaginning* ch. 51–53.

44.4 *manna*: A genitive of respect (see 7.1 and note).

44.6 *Fimbulvetr*: The horrendous and lengthy winter that will precede the Ragnarǫk and that Snorri (*Gylfaginning* ch. 51) describes in this way: *Mikil tíðendi eru þaðan at segja ok mǫrg. Þau in fyrstu at vetr sá kemr er kallaðr er fimbulvetr. Þá drífr snær ór ǫllum áttum. Frost eru þá mikil ok vindir hvassir. Ekki nýtr sólar. Þeir vetr fara þrír saman ok ekki sumar milli. En áðr gangi svá aðrir þrír vetr at þá er um alla verǫld orrustur miklar* ("There are many great things to say about that. The first is that that winter that is called Fimbulvetr will come. Then the snow will drive from all directions. The frosts will then be great, and the winds will be fierce. The sun will not shine at all. Three of those winters will come together, without any summer in between. But before them will be three other winters in which there will be very terrible battles throughout the world"). *Vǫluspá* does not mention the Fimbulvetr by name, though the reference to a *vindǫld* ("age of storms") at 45.9 may indicate that the poet knew of the myth.

45.1 *Líf oc Lífðrasir*: These names occur only here and in Snorri's quotation of this stanza in *Gylfaginning* ch. 53. The names mean "Life" and "Persistent Life" (an agent noun literally meaning "the one who fights for life") or, if derivation from *þrasa* ("to rage") is presumed, something like "raging or impetuous life." They are in any case transparently allegorical and suggest the survival of humankind after the Ragnarǫk. Though both names should be grammatically masculine, *þau* at 45.2 indicates that one (probably Líf) is intended as feminine; indeed, the survival of a male and female is consistent with the emphasis these stanzas place on regeneration. Læifþrasir in AR²W would mean something like "Persistent Remnant" or "Persistent Survival," and so also seems allegorically appropriate, although Finnur Jónsson (*Lexicon Poeticum*, s.v. *Lífþrasir*) considers it "certainly incorrect." Leidþrasir ("Persistent Way") in T is nonsensical in context and so must be a scribal error.

45.3 *í holti Hoddmimis*: Hoddmimir is mentioned only here and in Snorri's quotation of this stanza. *holldi* ("flesh") in A and U, as Ejder ("Eddadikten," 18–19) notes, is presumably due to anticipation of *d* in *Hoddmimis*, and *Ymis holdi* in 21.1 and Snorri's claim (*Gylfaginning* ch. 14) that dwarves originated in the earth like maggots in flesh can also be mentioned as potential sources of confusion. Gering (*Die Lieder*: Kom-

mentar, 175) speculates that Hoddmimir may be the name of the woods itself, rather than of an owner of the woods (cf. *Yggdrasils ascr* ["the ash Yggdrasill"] at *Vsp.* 47.1–2). In either case, the name is again transparently allegorical: a forest named "Treasure-Memory" would be a nurturing place (see *morgindǫggvar* in 45.4) that would thus both recall and predict prosperity.

45.4 *morgindǫggvar*: This post-Ragnarǫk food, mentioned as such only here and in Snorri's quotation, recalls the manna mentioned in Exodus 16:13–16: "And it came to pass, that at even the quails came up, and covered the camp: and in the morning the dew lay round about the host. And when the dew that lay was gone up, behold, upon the face of the wilderness there lay a small round thing, as small as the hoar frost on the ground. And when the children of Israel saw it, they said one to another, It is manna: for they wist not what it was. And Moses said unto them, This is the bread which the Lord hath given you to eat." Like *morgindǫggvar*, of course, manna is the food that enables the Israelites to survive their ordeal in the wilderness.

45.6 *þaðan af*: That is, from Líf and Lífðrasir new generations will arise, not from the *morgindǫggvar*.

46.1–2 *Fiǫlþ ... freistaþac*: Henceforth in both R and A Óðinn's questions are drastically abbreviated; R here reads *Fiolþ ec f. f. e. f. ;*. See note to 22.

46.4 *hvaðan*: The sense here is probably not "whence" but, as the answer in stanza 47 implies, "how." For this usage see *HHII* 9.2.

46.5 *slétta*: *sléttr* is used to describe the sky only here (Gering, *Die Lieder: Kommentar*, 176), though in scaldic verse the adjective modifies countries (Finnur Jónsson, *Lexicon Poeticum*, s.v.). The intended image is thus perhaps that of the post-Ragnarǫk world being a new land.

46.6 *þá*: *þá* in R completes a line, and when the scribe began the next line he accidentally wrote *þá* again. See the Textual Notes.

46.6 *Fenrir*: The Fenrir wolf, which will also devour Óðinn at the Ragnarǫk (53.1–2), is the wolf to whom the god Týr lost his hand. According to Snorri, Týr placed his hand in the wolf's mouth as security that should the wolf be unable to free himself from the chain Gleipnir, the gods would release him. They did not do so, whereupon Fenrir wolf bit off Týr's hand. The wolf was then fastened to the stone Þviti and his mouth was braced open with a sword. There, Snorri ominously observes, *liggr hann til ragnarøkrs*. See *Gylfaginning* ch. 25 and 34.

46.6 *farit*: Here probably in the sense "destroyed," though simply "overtaken" is also possible. When used with the former meaning, *fara* generally takes the dative (Cleasby and Vigfusson, *An Icelandic-English Dictionary*, s.v., sense B.2), and it is for this reason that at 47.3 U reads *henni*.

47.1 *dóttur*: In Germanic mythology, as opposed to classical, the sun is typically conceived of as female and the moon as male (*sól* is feminine and *máni* is masculine). This stanza is quoted in *Gylfaginning* ch. 53.

47.2 *Álfrǫðull*: This name is also used for the sun in *Skm.* 4.4–5: *þvíat álfrǫðull / lýsir um alla daga* ("because Álfroðull shines over all the days"). According to Snorri in *Gylfaginning* ch. 17, there are two types of elves: *ljósálfar*, who inhabit Álfheimr, and *døkkálfar*, who live *niðri í jǫrðu* ("down in the earth"). The former are *fegri en sól sýnum* ("fairer than the sun in appearance"). On elves in Old English as well as Old Norse, see Alaric Hall, *Elves in Anglo-Saxon England*.

47.4–6 *sú ... mær*: *sú* modifies *mær*, which is the subject of the sentence; *brautir* is the object: "When the gods die, that maiden must ride the ways of the mother." The image of the sun as riding in a chariot also appears in *Grm.* 37 and *Gylfaginning* ch. 11, where the chariot's horses are named Árvakr and Alsviðr. Also cf. stanza 12.

48.4 *ro*: Assimilation has reduced *hveriar ero* to *hveriar ro*.

48.4 *meyiar*: The precise identity of these "maidens" is obscure, as is, consequently, much of the rest of this stanza and also stanza 49. The words *fródgediaþar* and *hamingior*, in the context of a discussion of the new and better world to come, would seem to suggest that the *meyiar* are beneficent beings. They thus form a "very clear counterpart," in Boer's phrase (*Die Edda*, 2: 58), to the three *þursa meyiar* who are mentioned in *Vsp*. 8 as the harbingers, if not instigators, of the destruction of the world. Those *meyiar*, who are also known to Snorri (*Gylfaginning* ch. 14), will come *ór iǫtunheimom*, and so they cannot be the same as the eternal (if not always helpful) Norns (see further de Vries, *Altgermanische Religionsgeschichte*, 192–93, and Sigurður Nordal, *Vǫluspá*, 23–24). Boer suggests that Óðinn is here in a "poetic ecstasy" – presumably of the sort he experiences in *Grímnismál* – and that in visualizing the maidens cross the waves he is continuing a train of thought begun in stanza 44; along with Líf and Lífðrasir, that is, the maidens come from the new world. In *Heiðreks saga* ch. 10, Óðinn asks three riddles similar in form to the present question, and their answer is "waves" (Ruggerini, "A Stylistic and Typological Approach," 184–87). If *meyiar* here refers to waves, the following stanza would describe the inundation of the land by the sea in the final stages of the Ragnarǫk (see further below).

48.5 *mar*: This is presumably the sea that will cover the smoldering world after the Ragnarǫk and from which the earth, *iðiagræna* ("ever-green"), will rise again. See *Vsp*. 57–59. *líþa* thus probably signifies flight above, not across, the waters.

48.6 *fara*: The relative pronoun *er* should be understood before this verb.

49.1 *þióðar*: Bugge (*Sæmundar Edda*, 73) construes *þióðar* as a nominative modified by *Þriár*, but as Gering (*Die Lieder: Kommentar*, 177) notes, *þióðar* is unattested as a nominative form. Consequently, Finnur Jónsson (*De gamle Eddadigte*) and others emend to *þióðir*. As the manuscripts stand, *þióðar* is a partitive genitive predicated of *Þriár*. Reading the form as *þióðár* ("mighty rivers"), as Gering does, renders the passage still more obscure.

49.2 *falla ... yfir*: Literally "will fall over" but here in the sense "will come upon, enter"; *yfir* probably owes to the fact that the maidens are flying.

49.2 *þorp*: *þorp*, which is evidently plural here (see note to 49.4–5), implies villages or settlements as opposed to single farms or dwellings and is thus appropriate as a metaphor for the resettling of the world after the Ragnarǫk.

49.3 *Mǫgþrasis*: "Persistent Son" (an agent noun literally meaning "the one who fights for a son") is another obscure figure unique to *Vafþrúðnismál*. The element *þrasir* suggests that he may be related to *Lífðrasir*, and indeed Boer (*Die Edda*, 2: 58) contends that the two are one and the same: "as long as he remains concealed *í holti Hoddmimis* he is called Lífþrasir ... in the new world, which will be peopled with sons, he is called Mǫgþrasir." Though this identification is not required, Mǫgþrasir, like Líf and Lífðrasir, seems to be a symbolic name: "Persistent Son" seems an entirely appropriate name for the individual who, evidently, will found the new world after the Ragnarǫk. In Gering's reading (*Die Lieder: Kommentar*, 177), it makes the most sense to interpret *Mǫgþrasis* as being predicated of *þorp*, even if the syntax is a bit unusual. The "settlements of Mǫgþrasir" refers to the new, re-inhabited world, and 49.1–3 may thus be translated as "Three of the race of maidens will come over the settlements of Mǫgþrasir." Gering also suggests that stanzas 48 and 49 properly belong after stanza 45 and that such an arrangement would imply that Mǫgþrasir is the son of Lífðrasir. Alternatively, if *þioðar* is predicated of *þorp*, then *Mǫgþrasis* must relate to the maidens, so that the lines would mean "three of Mǫgþrasir's maidens will come over the settlements of the people (i.e. humankind)."

49.4–5 *hamingior ... ero*: The *hamingior* were guardian spirits similar to the *fylgjur* (see Cleasby and Vigfusson, *An Icelandic-English Dictionary*, s.v., and Turville-Petre, *Viga-Glúms Saga*, 64, and *Myth and Religion*, 227–

30). When *einar* is postposed, as it is here, it means "alone" or "only." *heimi* evidently refers to the new region – not one of the *nío heima* (43.5) – that will be inhabited after the Ragnarǫk. *þeira* cannot refer to the *meyiar* and be predicated of *hamingior*, for as semi-divine creatures the *meyiar* would not have guardian spirits. Nor would it seem to refer to the *meyiar* and be predicated of *heimi*, for the *meyiar* have not been associated with a specific *heimr*. *þeira* thus likely refers to the *þorp* that will be established in the new *heimr*, and if so *þorp* would be plural. In this reading, the sense of the line is "guardian spirits will be in the region of the settlements." In other words, the new world (*þorp*) will be a safe one for its inhabitants in which no malevolent spirits dwell. If the emendation *þióðir* is accepted in 49.1, *þeira* would refer to it; 49.1 would then mean "Three tribes of maidens," and 49.5 "will be in the homeland of those tribes." The problem with this interpretation is that a reference in 49.1 to several tribes would be an odd answer to a question about individual maidens.

49.6 *þó ... alaz:* *þær* cannot refer to the *hamingior*, who are unconnected with the giants, nor can it refer to *þorp*, which is neuter. It must, therefore, refer to the maidens (*Þriár* or *meyiar*). In *Vsp.* 8 the three destructive maidens who will presage the downfall of the gods *qvómo ... ór iǫtunheimom*, whence their beneficent counterparts are thus evidently presumed to originate as well.

50.6 *Surtalogi:* Here and the next stanza are the only places in which the fire that will destroy the world is clearly identified as Surtalogi (but see 17.6 and note), though the idea may underlie *Surtar ... sefi* ("Surtr's kinsman") in *Vsp.* 47.7–8. See Sigurður Nordal (*Vǫluspá*, 92–94). In *Gylfaginning* ch. 4 Snorri speaks of the *loganda sverð* ("burning sword") with which Surtr will conquer the gods, perhaps extrapolating from Genesis 3:24 or *Vsp.* 52.1–4: *Surtr ferr sunnan / með sviga lævi, / scínn af sverði / sól valtíva* ("Surtr will travel from the south with the bane of sticks [i.e. fire]; the sun of the gods of slaughter will shine from the sword"). See further Sigurður Nordal, *Vǫluspá*, 102–4.

51.1 *Víþarr oc Váli*: Viþarr's vengeance for Óðinn is described in *Vsp.* 55. Váli is not there mentioned, though *Vsp.* 32–33 notes how one of Óðinn's sons avenged Baldr, and *Bdr.* 11 explicitly declares that Váli will avenge the death of Baldr; *Vsp.* 34 may also contain a reference to Váli (see Sigurður Nordal, *Vǫluspá*, 70–71). Neither *Vǫluspá* nor *Gylfaginning*, however, suggests that Víþarr and Váli will be the rulers of Ásgarðr after the Ragnarǫk. *Vǫluspá* in fact states that the peace-loving Baldr and Hǫðr will return, and the story in *Vafþrúðnismál* may reflect a more martial tradition of life after the Ragnarǫk (cf. the references to Þórr's sons in the following stanza). See *Vsp.* 62–63 and *Gylfaginning* ch. 53, where this stanza is quoted.

51.2 *vé*: Literally, a *vé* would be a place marked off as sacred (cf. *vigja*, "to make sacred"), but precisely what a *vé* was (e.g. a temple or a field) is unclear. See Foote and Wilson (*The Viking Achievement*, 396–98).

51.3 *slocnar*: *sortnar* ("grows dark"), the reading of R²TW, is also possible and in fact recalls a similar passage in *Vsp.* 57.1–4: *Sól tér sortna / sígr fold í mar / hverfa af himni / heiðar stiǫrnor* ("The sun will begin to darken, the earth will sink into the sea, the bright stars will fall from the sky").

51.4 *Móþi oc Magni*: They are also identified as Þórr's sons in *Hym.* 34.1 and *Hrbl.* 9.6 and 53.4. Their inheritance of Þórr's famous hammer suggests that in the new world they will fulfill Þórr's various roles. Martin (*Ragnarǫk*, 135) notes, "The god who sustains life has fallen, and his sons renew the attributes of his power and the means of making them effective. The fact that they may be personifications of aspects of the god's nature and that their significance is only eschatological does not detract from the importance of their function in myth. The return of Magni and Móði after the fall of the gods means that the new order can be established."

51.6 *oc vinna*: Most editions follow AR²TW and read *Vingnis*, which would mean "The One Who Swings" and would refer to Þórr's use of Mjǫllnir; in *Þrk.* 1.1 and *Alv.* 6.1, by comparison, Þórr is called Vingþórr. *Vignigs synir* in U is the sort of alteration (presumably of Vingnis) that characterizes this manuscript. The reading of AR²TWU would mean that at the end of the battle Móði and Magni will get their father's hammer. The reading of R is the *lectio facilior* and so is very likely a scribal alteration of *Vingnis*. That is, when scribes intentionally altered the texts they were copying, they were more likely to simplify readings than to complicate them, and so in a pair of otherwise equally possible variants, the easier one is probably scribal. The reading of R would thus mean that Móði and Magni took up Mjǫllnir and assumed their father's place in general after the Miðgarðsormr killed him and subsequently performed (*vinna*) his duties in the battle in particular.

53.1–2 *Úlfr ... Aldafǫþr*: *Vsp.* 53.3–4 notes only that *Óðinn ferr / við úlf vega* ("Óðinn will go to fight against the wolf"), though Snorri, perhaps influenced by the present stanza, observes, *Úlfrinn gleypir Óðin*. Sigurður Nordal (*Vǫluspá*, 107) suggests that the poet of *Vǫluspá* knew the details of this legend – including Víþarr's breaking of the wolf's jaw, which he also does not mention (see 53.4–5 and note) – but that these "concepts [were] too tasteless and coarse for the author." Surviving in sculpture from both Scandinavia and England, the image may indeed have been well known (see Turville-Petre, *Myth and Religion*, plates 29 and 38).

53.3 *reca*: *vreca*, the earlier form of this word (cf. Gothic *wrikan* and OE *wrecan*), is necessary for alliteration, and most editors emend accordingly. Since [v] before [r] had probably disappeared in the pre-literary period of Norse (Noreen, *Altnordische Grammatik*, §288), the alliteration here suggests an early date for the poem. Cf. *Reiðgotom* at 12.5 and note. Fidjestøl argues that such forms point either to composition before 1000, to an East Norse origin, or to both (*The Dating of Eddic Poetry*, 231–45).

53.4–5 *kalda ... mun*: *kaldr* literally means "cold," but Dronke (*The Poetic Edda*, 1: 47) points out that in Old Norse "cold" "as an epithet for speech or counsel has the connotations 'sinister,' 'hostile,' 'fate-bring-ing.'" Cf. *Ls.* 51.6, *Akv.* 2.6, and *Vkv.* 31.6. *Vsp.* 55.5–8 mentions only that Víþarr will stab Fenrir near the heart, though Snorri (*Gylfaginning* ch. 51) observes, Víþarr *stígr ǫðrum fœti í neðra keypt úlfsins ... Annarri hendi tekr hann inn efra keypt úlfsins ok rífr sundr gin hans ok verðr þat úlfsins bani* ("will step with one foot on the lower jaw of the wolf ... With one hand he will take the upper jaw of the wolf and tear its mouth apart, and that will be the death of the wolf"). Snorri also notes that on Víþarr's foot will be a magic shoe that is continually being fashioned from the strips of leather shorn from the toes and heels of shoes. Sigurður Nordal (*Vǫluspá*, 107) suggests that "there must have been a folktale of Víðarr's vengeance, supported by the popular belief about his shoe," and indeed the belief that, until the Ragnarǫk, Fenrir wolf's jaw will be braced open with a sword would seem to invite the demise here described. See 46.6 and note.

53.6 *vitnis*: *Vingnis* in R has perhaps been intruded from the archetype at 51.6 (see note) and under the influence of the following *vigi*.

54.4–6 *hvat ... syni*: Having learned that Vafþrúðnir has no more information about Óðinn's fate than the god does – that Óðinn will in fact be killed at the Ragnarǫk – Óðinn asks a question differing in both structure and content from the preceding ones; it is presumably answerable only by Óðinn and Baldr and so has been calculated as a way to terminate the game. In *Heiðreks saga* the question is also the last in an exchange of riddles between the disguised Óðinn and King Heiðrekr. There the form is: *Hvat mælti Óðinn / í eyra Baldri / áðr hann væri á bál haðr?* While the final line itself lacks alliteration, this form of the question eliminates a number of problems that occur in the form found in *Vafþrúðnismál*: the awkward alliteration on *áþr*, the subjunctive mood of *stigi*, and the disjunction of the main clause. Because of the superior syntax of the riddle as it appears in *Heidreks saga*, Gering (*Die Lieder: Kommentar*, 179) contends that it is the older, original form. Gering further argues that the form in *Heiðreks saga* derives from a "better text" of *Vafþrúðnismál* than that of R on the grounds that Heiðrekr's answer, *Þat veiztu einn, rög vættr* ("You alone know that, perverted creature"), "is obviously a tendentious rearrangement of Vafþrúðnir's answer originating with a Christian author." Whether such a "rearrangement" would in fact render the form in *Heiðreks saga* superior to that in *Vafþrúðnismál* is not at all clear, however. And although *Heiðreks saga* in its present form certainly post-dates *Vafþrúðnismál*, the significance of the occurrence of this question in both texts remains problematic. Turville-Petre (*Hervarar saga og Heiðreks*, 82), for instance, suggests an ordering opposite to the one Gering proposes: "It [the question in *Heiðreks saga*] is probably derived from the last question which Óðinn puts to" Vafþrúðnir. Conversely, Holtsmark ("Den uløselige gåten," 102) argues that neither form is derived from the other, and Tolkien (*Hervarar saga ok Heiðreks konungs*, xx) speculates that the question may appear in the saga because even though it is not a riddle, it had become the "traditional unanswerable question." In any case, it is clear that in *Heiðreks saga*, as in *Vafþrúðnismál*, Óðinn intends to terminate the contest with this question, for he begins the stanza with *Segðu þat þá hinzt* ("Say this last of all").

54.5–6 *áþr ... syni*: The syntax is elliptical, and *sonr* must be understood in 54.5; *siálfr* in 54.6 refers to Óðinn.

55.1 *Ey ... veit*: *Ey* properly means "always," though the form is also a contraction of *ei-gi*, meaning "never," and such may be the case here (see Cleasby and Vigfusson, *An Icelandic-English Dictionary*, s.v. *ei*, sense 2). Both Cleasby-Vigfusson (sense 3) and Finnur Jónsson (*Lexicon Poeticum*, s.v. 3 *ey*) also record the word as a negative particle, but in each case the only unambiguous example is the present occurrence. *manne* in R is evidently a dative (cf. *manni* in A), though this particular inflectional spelling occurs nowhere else in *Vafþrúðnismál* (see further Noreen, *Altnordische Grammatik*, §145). Noreen (§318.5) speculates that *manne* here may be a nominative corresponding to Gothic *manna*, yet this identification seems philologically very unlikely. Neckel ("Zu den germanischen Negationen," 6) suggests that *Ey manne* is a scribal corruption of *Ey mann né* or *Ey mannr né*, but if this analysis clarifies the usage of *Ey*, it does not facilitate interpretation of *veit*. Indeed, the impersonal usage for the active voice of *vita* is required here, but as Gering (*Die Lieder: Kommentar*, 179) points out, such a usage is hard to explain and surprising; there is a similar apparently impersonal usage at *Ls.* 19.4, though these lines are also obscure. *veit* may also simply be a scribal error for *veizk*. The sense, in any case, is "That is known to no man."

55.2 *hvat þú*: It is often argued (e.g. Gering, *Die Lieder: Kommentar*, 179; cf. Kragerud, "De mytologiske spørsmål," 35) that *hvat* Óðinn said is that Váli will avenge Baldr and that Baldr will return after the Ragnarøk, but the point of the question, as Holtsmark ("Den uløselige gåten," 104–5) notes, is that only Óðinn knows its answer. It is central to *Vafþrúðnismál* as a fictional work, she suggests, that neither Vafþrúðnir nor the audience should have any way of knowing anything besides what Óðinn actually says in the poem; otherwise, Óðinn would not be *æ vísastr*. It is also noteworthy that *þú* implies Vafþrúðnir's immediate recognition of his adversary's identity. The nature of the question (its calculation as well as its unanswerability) similarly enables King Heiðrekr to recognize that his opponent is Óðinn (see note to 54.4–6). In each case, Ejder ("Eddadikten," 14–15) points out, Óðinn's question about himself foreshadows the conclusion. In *Bdr.* 13 the witch also recognizes Óðinn at the end of the poem, though why this particular question (about weeping maidens) precipitates this recognition is not as clear. It is perhaps significant that for this question, as for Óðinn's last question in *Vafþrúðnismál*, no answer has yet achieved scholarly consensus.

55.2 *í árdaga*: Finnur Jónsson (*De gamle Eddadigte*, 62) notes that the phrase implies a long time has passed since Baldr's death, and it may be that the poet has included this emphasis, in conjunction with Óðinn's concern about his own fate, in order to suggest that the Ragnarøk is at hand.

55.7–9 nú ... vera: Finnur Jónsson (*De gamle Eddadigte*, 62) regards these lines as a "weak and artificial addition," but Boer suggests that the expanded stanza length gives the poem a "solemn conclusion", as is the case with the final spell of *Hv.* 163. Phillpotts (*The Elder Edda*, 105) argues, rather tendentiously, that it "is obviously implied that the scene ends with the giant's death at the hands of Odin, and we should expect the commentator to supply us with a prose account of this, somewhat as the prose at the end of *Grímnismál* tells of Geirröð's death. But the dramatic catastrophe has apparently escaped his attention." *deildac mína orþspeci* essentially means "I spoke," though the sense "I shared my wisdom" also is appropriate. Cf. *Rþ.* 45.1–2: *Hann við Ríg iarl / runar deildi* ("He 'divided mysteries' with earl Ríg"). Also cf. *freista orþspeci* at 5.2. *vera* is probably the genitive plural of *verr*, here in the sense "male beings." Cf. *Hym.* 15.5, where *Sifiar verr* is used for Þórr. The sense is thus that Óðinn is the wisest of all creatures – men, giants, and gods.

BIBLIOGRAPHY

Facsimiles, Editions, Translations

Auden, W.H., and Paul B. Taylor, trans. *Norse Poems*. London: Athlone Press, 1981.

Boer, R.C., ed. *Die Edda mit historisch-kritischem Commentar*. 2 vols. Haarlem: H.D. Tjeenk Willink & zoon, 1922.

Bugge, Sophus, ed. *Norrœn Fornkvæði: Islandsk Samling af folkelige Oldtidsdigte om Nordens Guder og Heroer almindelig kaldet Sæmundar Edda hins fróða*. Christiania: P.T. Malling, 1867; rpt. Oslo: Universitetsforlaget, 1965.

Detter, F., and R. Heinzel, ed. *Sæmundar Edda: Mit einem Anhang*. 2 vols. in 1. Leipzig: G. Wigand, 1903.

Dronke, Ursula, ed. *The Poetic Edda*. Vol. 1: *Heroic Poems*. Oxford: Clarendon Press, 1969.

—, ed. *The Poetic Edda*. Vol. 2: *Mythological Poems*. Oxford: Clarendon Press, 1997.

Faulkes, Anthony, ed. *Codex Trajectinus: The Utrecht Manuscript of the Prose Edda*. Early Icelandic Manuscripts in Facsimile 15. Copenhagen: Rosenkilde & Bagger, 1985.

—, trans. *Edda*, by Snorri Sturluson. Everyman Classics. Everyman's Library 499. London: Dent, 1987.

—, ed. *Edda: Prologue and Gylfaginning*, by Snorri Sturluson. Oxford: Clarendon Press; New York: Oxford University Press, 1982.

Finnur Jónsson, ed. *De gamle Eddadigte*. Copenhagen: G.E.C. Gad, 1932.

Gering, Hugo, ed. *Die Lieder der Edda*. Vol. 3: *Kommentar*. Ed. B. Sijmons. Germanistische Handbibliothek 7.3. Halle: Buchhandlung des Waisenhauses, 1927.

Grape, Anders, ed. *Snorre Sturlasons Edda, Uppsala-håndskriften DG 11*. 2 vols. Stockholm: Almqvist & Wiksell, 1962–1977.

Guðni Jónsson, ed. *Fornaldarsögur Norðurlanda.* 4 vols. Reykjavík: Íslendingasagnaútgáfan, 1950.

Heusler, Andreas, ed. *Codex Regius of The Elder Edda.* Corpus Codicum Islandicorum Medii Aevi 10. Copenhagen: Levin & Munksgaard, 1937.

Hildebrand, Karl, ed. *Die Lieder der älteren Edda (Sæmundar Edda).* 3rd ed. by Hugo Gering. Bibliothek der ältesten deutschen Litteratur-Denkmäler 7. Paderborn: F. Schöningh, 1912.

Hill, Joyce, ed. *Old English Minor Heroic Poems.* Durham and St Andrews Medieval Texts 4. Durham: Durham and St Andrews Medieval Texts, 1983. 2nd ed. Durham: Centre for Mediaeval and Renaissance Studies; Toronto: Pontifical Institute of Mediaeval Studies, forthcoming.

Jón Helgason, ed. *Eddadigte.* Vol. 2: *Gudedigte.* Nordisk filologi. Tekster og lærebøger til universitetsbrug, Serie A, 7. 2nd ed. Copenhagen: Munksgaard, 1962.

—, ed. *Tvær kviður fornar: Völundarkviða og Atlakviða med skýringum.* 3rd ed. Reykjavik: Heimskringla, 1966.

La Farge, Beatrice, and John Tucker. *Glossary to the "Poetic Edda": based on Hans Kuhn's Kurzes Wörterbuch.* Skandinavistische Arbeiten 15. Heidelberg: Carl Winter, 1992.

Larrington, Carolyne, trans. *The Poetic Edda.* World's Classics. Oxford; New York: Oxford University Press, 1996.

Neckel, Gustav, ed. *Edda: Die Lieder des Codex regius nebst verwandten Denkmälern.* Germanische Bibliothek 4. 4th ed. by Hans Kuhn. Heidelberg: C. Winter, 1962–1968.

Nordal, Sigurður, ed. *Codex Wormianus (The Younger Edda)*, by Snorri Sturluson. Corpus Codicum Islandicorum Medii Aevi 2. Copenhagen: Levin & Munksgaard, 1931.

—, ed. *Vǫluspá.* Trans. B.S. Benedikz and John McKinnell. Durham and St Andrews Medieval Texts 1. Durham: Durham and St Andrews Medieval Texts, 1978.

Sijmons, B., ed. *Die Lieder der Edda.* Vol. 1: *Text.* Germanistische Handbibliothek 7.1. Halle: Buchhandlung des Waisenhauses, 1906.

Terry, Patricia, trans. *Poems of the Vikings; The Elder Edda*. Indianapolis: Bobbs-Merrill, 1969.

Tolkien, Christopher, ed. *Hervarar saga ok Heiðreks konungs*. Icelandic Texts. London; New York: Nelson, 1960.

Turville-Petre, Gabriel, ed. *Hervarar saga og Heiðreks*. Introduction by Christopher Tolkien. Viking Society for Northern Research 2. London: Viking Society for Northern Research, University College, 1956.

—, ed. *Víga-Glúms saga*. 2nd ed. Oxford: Clarendon Press, 1960.

Wessén, Elias, ed. *Codex Regius to The Younger Edda*, by Snorri Sturluson. Corpus Codicum Islandicorum Medii Aevi 14. Copenhagen: E. Munksgaard, 1940.

—, ed. *Fragments of The Elder and The Younger Edda*. Corpus Codicum Islandicorum Medii Aevi 17. Copenhagen: E. Munksgaard, 1945.

—, ed. *Ynglingasaga*, by Snorri Sturluson. Nordisk filologi. Tekster og lærebøker til universitetsbruk, Serie A, 6. Oslo: Dreyers, 1976.

Secondary Criticism

Ármann Jakobsson. "A Contest of Cosmic Fathers: God and Giant in *Vafþrúðnismál*." *Neophilologus* 92 (2008): 263–77.

—. "Where Do the Giants Live?" *Arkiv för nordisk filologi* 121 (2006): 101–12.

Bæksted, Anders. *Islands Runeindskrifter*. Bibliotheca Arnamagnæana 2. Copenhagen: Ejnar Munksgaard, 1942.

Barnes, Michael, and Anthony Faulkes. *A New Introduction to Old Norse*. 4th ed. London: Viking Society for Northern Research, 2007.

Bax, Marcel, and Tineke Padmos. "Two Types of Verbal Dueling in Old Icelandic: The Interactional Structure of the *senna* and the *mannjafnaðr* in *Hárbarðsljóð*." *Scandinavian Studies* 55 (1983): 149–74.

Bugge, Sophus. *Der Runenstein von Rök in Östergötland, Schweden*. Stockholm: Haeggström, 1910.

Chadwick, H.M. *The Cult of Othin: An Essay in the Ancient Religion of the North*. London: C.J. Clay, 1899.

Christiansen, Hallfrid. "Det norrøne ord lúðr." *Maal og Minne* (1952): 101–6.

Cleasby, Richard, and Gudbrand Vigfusson. *An Icelandic-English Dictionary*. 2nd ed. by Sir William Craigie. Oxford: Clarendon Press, 1957.

Clover, Carol J. "The Germanic Context of the Unferþ Episode." *Speculum* 55 (1980): 444–68.

—. "*Hárbarðsljóð* as Generic Farce." *Scandinavian Studies* 51 (1979): 124–45.

Dörner, Hans Helmut. "Die 'Vafþrúðnismál' als Heilsbotschaft im Germanischen Heidentum." *Amsterdamer Beiträge zur älteren Germanistik* 51 (1999): 67–79.

DuBois, Thomas A. *Nordic Religions in the Viking Age*. The Middle Ages Series. Philadelphia: University of Pennsylvania Press, 1999.

Dumézil, Georges. *Gods of the Ancient Northmen*. Ed. and trans. Einar Haugen. Introduction by C. Scott Littleton and Udo Strutynski. UCLA Center for the Study of Comparative Folklore and Mythology Publications 3. Berkeley: University of California Press, 1973.

Einar Ól. Sveinsson. *Íslenzkar bókmenntir í fornöld* 1. Reykjavík: Almenna bókafélagið, 1962.

—. "Kormakr the Poet and His Verses." *Saga-Book: Viking Society for Northern Research* 17 (1966–69): 18–60.

Ejder, Bertil. "Eddadikten Vafþrúðnismál." *Vetenskaps Societeten i Lund Årsbok* (1960): 5–20.

Ellis (Davidson), Hilda Roderick. *Gods and Myths of Northern Europe*. Pelican book A670. Harmondsworth; Baltimore: Penguin, 1964.

—. "Insults and Riddles in the *Edda* Poems." In *Edda: A Collection of Essays*, ed. Robert J. Glendinning and Haraldur Bessason, pp. 25–46. University of Manitoba Icelandic Studies 4. Manitoba: University of Manitoba Press, 1983.

—. *The Road to Hel: A Study of the Conception of the Dead in Old Norse Literature*. Cambridge: Cambridge University Press, 1943.

Faulkes, Anthony. "Edda." *Gripla* 2 (1977): 32–9.

Fidjestøl, Bjarne. *The Dating of Eddic Poetry: A Historical Survey and Methodological Investigation*. Ed. Odd Einar Haugen. Bibliotheca Arnamagnæana 41. Copenhagen: Reitzel, 1999.

Finnur Jónsson. *Lexicon poeticum antiquae linguae septentrionalis*. 2nd ed. Copenhagen: S.L. Møller, 1931.

—. *Den oldnorske og oldislandske litteraturs historie*, vol. 1. 2nd ed. Copenhagen: G.E.C. Gad, 1920.

—. "Om overleveringsdubletter." *Arkiv för nordisk filologi* 21 (1905): 1–14.

Foote, P.G., and D.M. Wilson. *The Viking Achievement: The Society and Culture of Early Medieval Scandinavia*. 2nd ed. Great Civilizations Series. London: Sidgwick & Jackson, 1980.

Gordon, E.V. *An Introduction to Old Norse*. 2nd ed. by A.R. Taylor. Oxford: Clarendon Press, 1957.

Gunnell, Terry. *The Origins of Drama in Scandinavia*. Woodbridge, UK: D.S. Brewer; Rochester, NY: Boydell & Brewer, 1995.

Hall, Alaric. *Elves in Anglo-Saxon England: matters of belief, health, gender and identity*. Anglo-Saxon Studies 8. Woodbridge, UK; Rochester, NY: Boydell, 2007.

Hallberg, Peter. *Old Icelandic Poetry: Eddic Lay and Skaldic Verse*. Trans. Paul Schach and Sonja Lindgrenson. Lincoln: University of Nebraska Press, 1975.

Harris, Joseph. "Eddic Poetry." In *Old Norse-Icelandic Literature: A Critical Guide*, ed. Carol J. Clover and John Lindow, pp. 68–156. Islandica 45. Ithaca: Cornell University Press, 1985.

Haugen, Einar. "The *Edda* as Ritual: Odin and His Masks." In *Edda: A Collection of Essays*, ed. Robert J. Glendinning and Haraldur Bessason, pp. 3–24. University of Manitoba Icelandic studies 4. Manitoba: University of Manitoba Press, 1983.

Heusler, Andreas. *Die altgermanische Dichtung*. 2nd ed. Handbuch der Literaturwissenschaft. Darmstadt: H. Gentner, 1957.

Holtsmark, Anne. "Det norrøne ord lúðr." *Maal og Minne* (1946): 49–65.

—. "Den uløselige gåten." *Maal og Minne* (1964): 101–5.

—. "Vafþrúðnismál." In *Kulturhistorisk Leksikon for nordisk middelalder* 19, ed. Johannes Brøndsted, John Danstrup, and Lis Rubin Jacobsen, pp. 422–23. Copenhagen: Rosenkilde & Bagger, 1975.

Jón Helgason. "Norges og Islands Digtning." In *Litteratur-historie B: Norge og Island*, ed. Sigurður Nordal. *Nordisk kultur* 8:B. Stockholm: A. Bonnier, 1953.

Kellogg, Robert. "The Prehistory of Eddic Poetry." In *Poetry in the Scandinavian Middle Ages: The Seventh International Saga Conference*, pp. 187–99. Spoleto: Presso la sede del Centro Studi (Centro italiano di studi sull'alto Medioevo), 1990.

Kershaw, Kris [Priscilla K.]. *The One-Eyed God: Odin and the (Indo-) Germanic Männerbünde*. Journal of Indo-European studies 36. Washington, DC: Institute for the Study of Man, 2000.

Klingenberg, Heinz. *Edda: Sammlung und Dichtung*. Beiträge zur nordischen Philologie 3. Basel: Helbing & Lichtenhahn, 1974.

Kock, Axel. "Ordforskning i den äldre Eddan." *Arkiv för nordisk filologi* 27 (1911): 107–40.

Kock, Ernst A. *Notationes Norroenae: Anteckningar till Edda och skaldediktning*. 28 vols. Lunds universitets årsskrift N.F. Lund: C.W.K. Gleerup, 1923–44.

Kragerud, Alv. "De mytologiske spørsmål i Fåvnesmål." *Arkiv för nordisk filologi* 96 (1981): 9–48.

Kuhn, Hans. "Zur Grammatik und Textgestaltung der älteren Edda." *Zeitschrift für deutsches Altertum* 90 (1960–61): 241–68.

—. "Die norwegischen Spuren in der Liederedda." *Acta Philologica Scandinavica* 22 (1952–4): 65–80.

Läffler, L. Fr. "Om några underarter av Ljóðaháttr." *Studier i nordisk filologi* 4 (1913): 1–124.

Larrington, Carolyne. *A Store of Common Sense: Gnomic Theme and Style in Old Icelandic and Old English Wisdom Poetry*. Oxford: Clarendon Press; Oxford; New York: Oxford University Press, 1993.

—. "*Vafþrúðnismál* and *Grímnismál*: Cosmic History, Cosmic Geography." In *The Poetic Edda: Essays on Old Norse Mythology*, ed. Paul Acker and Carolyne Larrington, pp. 62–77. Routledge Medieval Casebooks. London: Routledge, 2002.

Lassen, Annette. "Gud eller djævel? Kristningen af Odin." *Arkiv för nordisk filologi* 121 (2006): 121–38.

Lehmann, Winfred P. "The Composition of Eddic Verse." In *Studies in Germanic Languages and Literatures in Memory of Fred O. Nolte*, ed. Erich Hofacker and Liselotte Dieckman, pp. 7–14. St Louis: Washington University Press, 1963.

Liestøl, Aslak. "Runer frå Bryggen." *Viking* 27 (1964): 5–53; rev. as "Rúnavísur frá Björgvin," *Skirnir* 139 (1965): 27–51.

Lindblad, Gustaf. "Centrala eddaproblem i 1970–talets forsknings läge." *Scripta Islandica* 28 (1977): 3–26.

—. "Poetiska Eddans förhistoria och skrivskicket i Codex regius." *Arkiv för nordisk filologi* 95 (1980): 142–67.

—. "Snorre Sturlasson och eddadiktningen." *Saga och sed* (1978): 17–34.

—. *Studier i Codex regius av äldre Eddan.* Lundastudier i nordisk språkvetenskap 10. Lund: C.W.K. Gleerup, 1954.

Lindow, John. *Handbook of Norse Mythology.* Handbooks of World Mythology. Santa Barbara, CA: ABC–CLIO, 2001.

—. "Myth Read as History: Odin in Snorri Sturluson's *Ynglinga Saga*." In *Myth: A New Symposium*, ed. Gregory Schrempp and William Hansen, pp. 107–23. Bloomington: Indiana University Press, 2002.

—. "Mythology and Mythography." In *Old Norse-Icelandic Literature: A Critical Guide*, ed. Carol J. Clover and John Lindow, pp. 21–67. Islandica 45. Ithaca: Cornell University Press, 1985.

Lönnroth, Lars. "*Iǫrð fannz æva né upphiminn.* A Formula Analysis." In *Specvlvm Norroenvm*, pp. 310–27.

—. "Hjálmar's Death-Song and the Delivery of Eddic Poetry." *Speculum* 46 (1971): 1–20.

Lord, Albert B. *The Singer of Tales.* Harvard Studies in Comparative Literature 24. Cambridge, MA: Harvard University Press, 1960; rpt. New York: Atheneum, 1978.

Machan, Tim William. "Alliteration and the Editing of Eddic Poetry." *Scandinavian Studies* 64 (1992): 216–27.

Martin, John Stanley. "*Ár vas alda*. Ancient Scandinavian Creation Myths Reconsidered." In *Specvlvm Norroenvm*, pp. 357–69.

—. *Ragnarǫk: An Investigation into Old Norse Concepts of the Fate of the Gods*. Melbourne Monographs in Germanic Studies 3. Assen: Van Gorcum, 1972.

McKinnell, John. "Late Heathen Views of the World: 1. *Vafþrúðnismál*." In J. McKinnell and Maria Elena Ruggerini, *Both One and Many: Essays on Change and Variety in Late Norse Heathenism*, pp. 87–106. Philologia 1. Rome: Il Calamo, 1994.

—, Rudolf Simek, and Klaus Düwel. *Runes, Magic and Religion: A Sourcebook*. Studia Medievalia Septentrionalia 10. Vienna: Fassbaender, 2004.

Motz, Lotte. "Gods and Demons of the Wilderness: A Study in Norse Tradition." *Arkiv för nordisk filologi* 99 (1984): 175–87.

—. "Óðinn's Vision." *Maal og Minne* (1998): 11–19.

Neckel, Gustav. "Zu den germanischen Negationen." *Zeitschrift für vergleichende Sprachforschung* 45 (1913): 1–23.

Niepokuj, Mary. "Requests for a Hearing in Norse and Other Indo-European Languages." *Journal of Indo-European Studies* 25 (1997): 49–78.

Nordal, Sigurður. "Three Essays on *Völuspá*." Trans. B.S. Benedikz and J.S. McKinnell. *Saga-Book: Viking Society for Northern Research* 18 (1970–73): 79–135.

Noreen, Adolf. *Altnordische Grammatik*. Vol. 1: *Altisländische und altnorwegische Grammatik (Laut- und Flexionslehre) unter Berücksichtigung des Urnordischen*. 4th ed. 1923; rpt. Tubingen: M. Niemeyer, 1970 [cited by paragraph].

O'Donoghue, Heather. *From Asgard to Valhalla: The Remarkable History of the Norse Myths*. London: I.B. Tauris, 2007.

Olrik, Axel. *Om Ragnarok*. 2 vols. Copenhagen: G.E.C. Gad, 1902–14.

Ólsen, Björn Magnússon. "Til Eddakvadene II: Til Hávamál." *Arkiv för nordisk filologi* 31 (1915): 52–95.

—. "Til Eddakvadene III: Til Vafþrúðnismál." *Arkiv för nordisk filologi* 38 (1922): 195–6.

Olsen, Magnus. *Edda- og skaldekvad: Forarbeider til kommentar.* Vol. 7: *Gudedikte.* Avhandlinger utgitt av Det Norske Videnskaps-Akademi i Oslo 2. Hist.-Filos. Klasse, N.S. 5. Oslo: Universitetsforlaget, 1964.

—. "Til Rök-indskriften." *Arkiv för nordisk filologi* 37 (1921): 201–32.

Olsen, Olaf. *Hørg, Hov og Kirke: Historiske og arkæologiske Vikingetidsstudier.* Aarbøger for Nordisk Oldkyndighed og Historie. Copenhagen: G.E.C. Gad, 1966.

Page, R.I. "Dumézil Revisited." *Saga-Book: Viking Society for Northern Research* 20 (1978–79): 49–69.

Phillpotts, Bertha S. *The Elder Edda and Ancient Scandinavian Drama.* Cambridge: Cambridge University Press, 1920.

Quinn, Judy. "Dialogue with a *vǫlva*: *Vǫluspá, Baldrs draumar* and *Hyndluljóð.*" In *The Poetic Edda: Essays on Old Norse Mythology,* ed. Paul Acker and Carolyne Larrington, pp. 248–74. Routledge Medieval Casebooks. London: Routledge, 2002.

Reichardt, Konstantin. "A Contribution to the Interpretation of Skaldic Poetry: Tmesis." In *Old Norse Literature and Mythology: A Symposium,* ed. Edgar C. Polomé, pp. 200–26. Austin: University of Texas Press, 1969.

Ross, Margaret Clunies. *A History of Old Norse Poetry and Poetics.* Cambridge; New York: D.S. Brewer, 2005.

—. *Prolonged Echoes: Old Norse Myths in Medieval Northern Society.* 2 vols. Viking Collection 7, 10. Odense: Odense University Press, 1994, 1998.

Ruggerini, Maria Elena. "A Stylistic and Typological Approach to *Vafþrúðnismál.*" In John McKinnell and M.E. Ruggerini, *Both One and Many: Essays on Change and Variety in Late Norse Heathenism,* pp. 139–87. Philologia 1. Rome: Il Calamo, 1994.

Salberger, Evert. "Heill þú farir! Ett textproblem i Vafþrúðnismál 4." *Scripta Islandica* 25 (1974–75): 23–30.

—. "Ett stavrimsproblem i Vafþrúðnismál 34." *Maal og Minne* (1955): 113–20.

Salus, Peter H. "More 'Eastern Echoes' in the *Edda?* An Addendum." *MLN: Modern Language Notes* 79 (1964): 426–28.

Schier, Kurt. "Zur Mythologie der *Snorra Edda*: Einige Quellenprobleme." In *Specvlvm Norroenvm*, pp. 405–20.

Seip, Didrik Arup. "Har nordmenn skrevet opp Edda-diktningen?" *Maal og Minne* (1951): 3–33.

——. "Om et norsk skriftlig grunnlag for Edda-diktningen eller deler av den." *Maal og Minne* (1957): 81–195.

——. "On the Original of the Codex Regius of the Elder Edda." In *Studies in Honor of Albert Morey Sturtevant*, pp. 103–6. Humanistic Studies 29. Lawrence, KY: University of Kansas Press, 1952.

Specvlvm Norroenvm: Norse Studies in Memory of Gabriel Turville-Petre. Ed. Ursula Dronke, Guðrún P. Helgadóttir, Gerd Wolfgang Weber, and Hans Bekker-Nielsen. Odense: Odense University Press, 1981.

Söderberg, Barbro. "Formelgods och Eddakronologi." *Arkiv för nordisk filologi* 101 (1986): 50–86.

Sprenger, Ulrike. "*Vafðrúðnismál* 10.3: Der Kaltgerippte." In *Arbeiten zur Skandinavistik 6: Arbeitstagung der Skandinavisten des deutschen Sprachgebietes, 26.9.–1.10.1983 in Bonn*, ed. Heinrich Beck, pp. 185–210. Texte und Untersuchungen zur Germanistik und Skandinavistik 11. Frankfurt; New York: Lang, 1985.

Stefán Einarsson. *A History of Icelandic Literature*. New York: Johns Hopkins Press for the American-Scandinavian Foundation, 1957.

Stefán Karlsson. "Om norvagismer i islandske håndskrifter." *Maal og Minne* (1978): 87–101.

Steffensen, Jón. "Hugleiðingar um Eddukvæði." *Árbók hins íslenzka fornleifafélags* (1968): 26–38.

Swenson, Karen. *Performing Definitions: Two Genres of Insult in Old Norse Literature*. Columbia, SC: Camden House, 1991.

Tolley, Clive. "Sources for Snorri's Depiction of Óðinn in *Ynglinga Saga*: Lappish Shamanism and the *Historia Norvegiae*." *Maal og Minne* (1996): 67–79.

Turville-Petre, Gabriel. "The Cult of Óðinn in Iceland." In Gabriel Turville-Petre, *Nine Norse Studies*, pp. 1–19. Viking Society for Northern Research 5. London: University College, 1972.

—. "Fertility of Beast and Soil in Old Norse Literature." In *Old Norse Literature and Mythology*: *A Symposium*, ed. Edgar C. Polomé, pp. 244–64. Austin: University of Texas Press, 1969.

—. *Myth and Religion of the North*: *The Religion of Ancient Scandinavia*. London: Weidenfeld and Nicolson, 1964.

—. "Professor Dumézil and the Literature of Iceland." In *Hommages à Georges Dumézil*, pp. 209–14. Collection Latomus 45. Brussels: Revue d'études latines, 1960.

—. *Scaldic Poetry*. Oxford: Clarendon Press, 1976.

Valfells, Sigrid, and James E. Cathey. *Old Icelandic*: *An Introductory Course*. Oxford: Oxford University Press in association with the American-Scandinavian Foundation, 1981.

de Vries, Jan. *Altgermanische Religionsgeschichte*. 2 vols. 2nd ed. Berlin: de Gruyter, 1956–7.

—. *Altnordische Literaturgeschichte*. 2 vols. 2nd ed. Grundriss der germanischen Philologie 15–16. Berlin: de Gruyter, 1964–7.

—. *Altnordisches etymologisches Wörterbuch*. 2nd ed. Leiden: E.J. Brill, 1962.

—. "Om Eddaens Visdomsdigtning." *Arkiv för nordisk filologi* 50 (1934): 1–59.

Würth, Stefanie. "Ragnarök: Götterdämmerung und Weltende in der nordischen Literatur." *Jahrbuch der Oswald von Wolkenstein Gesellschaft* 13 (2001): 29–43.

GLOSSARY

The entries are arranged alphabetically, but long and short varieties of a given vowel are separated as they are in Modern Icelandic. Except for Ð, which follows D, the graphs not utilized in English are grouped at the end of the alphabet in accordance with Icelandic procedure: Þ, Æ, Œ, Ø, and Q. Every occurrence of every word is recorded, and several cross-references are included. Students should recall that the orthography of R, upon which this edition and, necessarily, this glossary are based, is irregular and should locate a desired word accordingly. When variant spellings exist in *Vafþrúðnismál*, words are listed under the form that is most common (e.g. *fjǫlþ*, but *ráða*). Definitions are intended for the words as they occur in *Vafþrúðnismál* alone, and the interested student should consult the standard dictionaries for further information. For entries that are semantically or philologically problematic, the reader is referred to an Explanatory Note. In the Index of Names, which follows the Glossary, literal translations of the less common names and places are enclosed in inverted commas.

AF, prep., from, out of: 1) with dat., 8.2, 9.2, 12.6, 37.4; 2) abs., as adv., 45.6

AFI, m., grandfather: nom. sg. afi, 29.6

ALA, str. v., to bear, nourish: md. 3 pers. pl. pres. alaz, 45.6, 49.6; pret. part. str. m. nom. sg. alinn, 38.8

ALDAR, ALDIR: *see* QLD

ALDRDAGAR, m. pl., "life-days," forever: acc. aldrdaga, 16.5

ALDRLAG, n., destruction: dat. sg. aldrlagi, 52.5

ALLR, adj., all: str. n. nom. sg. allt, 31.6 (note); str. m. nom. pl. allir, 41.1; str. f. nom. pl. allar, 31.5; str. m. acc. pl. alla, 37.6; str. n. acc. pl. qll, 38.3, 42.3; str. n. gen. pl. allra, 42.5, 43.2

AL(L)SVINNR, adj., extremely wise: wk. m. nom. sg. allsvinni, 42.7; wk. m. acc. sg. alsvinna, 1.6; wk. m. gen. sg. alsvinna, 5.3

ALLZ, conj., since, inasmuch as, 1.2, 11.2, 13.2, 15.2, 17.2, 24.2, 26.2, 28.2, 30.2, 32.2, 34.2, 36.2, 38.2

ALSVIÞR, adj., extremely wise (variant of al(l)svinnr, q.v.): str. m. nom. sg. alsviþr, 6.6, 34.6

ANDFANG, n., reception, hospitality: gen. pl. andfanga, 8.6

ANNARR, ord. number, second(ly): str. n. acc. sg. annat, 22.1

APTR, adv., back, back again, 4.2, 39.5

ARNAR: *see* QRN

AT, 1) prep., with dat., to, according to, as, upon, at: 5.4, 17.5, 18.2, 23.6, 25.6, 39.3, 45.5, 51.6, 52.5, 53.6; 2) particle with inf., to, 1.3, 5.2; 3) conj. introducing a subordinate clause, that, such that, 10.5, 22.5, 36.5

ATALL, adj., terrible, fierce: str. n. nom. sg. atalt, 31.6

AUSTAN, adv., from the east, 13.5

AUÞIGR, adj., wealthy, powerful: str. m. gen. sg. auþigs, 10.2 (used substantively – a wealthy man)

Á, prep.: 1) with acc., towards, upon, into, 6.3, 18.5, 19.2, 35.6, 46.5, 54.5; 2) with dat., on, at, 4.3, 7.3 (note), 11.2, 13.2, 15.2, 16.6, 17.2, 37.2; with respect to, concerning, 1.5

Á, f., river: nom. sg. á, 15.4, 16.1; dat. sg. á, 16.6

ÁRDAGAR, m. pl., days of old: acc. árdaga, 28.6, 55.2

ÁRTAL, n., year-reckoning: dat. sg. ártali, 23.6, 25.6

ÁSS, m., god: nom. pl. æsir, 50.4; gen. pl. ása, 28.4, 38.5; dat. pl. ásom, 38.8

ÁTTI: *see* EIGA

ÁTTI, ord. number, eighth: wk. n. acc. sg. átta, 34.1

ÁÞR, conj., before, 29.2, 35.2, 47.3, 54.5

BALDINN, adj., defiant, brave: wk. m. nom. sg. baldni, 32.5

BARN, n., child: acc. pl. bǫrn, 32.4

BÁL, n., flame, funeral pyre: acc. sg. bál, 54.5

BECCR, m., bench: acc. sg. becc, 19.2

BEIN, n., bone: dat. pl. beinom, 21.3

BERA, str. v., to bear, give birth to: 3 pers. pres. sg. berr, 47.2; pret. part. str. m. nom. sg. borinn, 29.3, 35.3; pret. part. str. f. nom. sg. borin, 25.3

BEZTR: *see* GÓÐR

BIARG, n., rock, stone: nom. pl. biǫrg, 21.3

BRAUT, f., road, way: acc. pl. brautir, 47.6

BYGGIA, wk. v., to inhabit, build: 3 pers. pl. pres. byggia, 51.2

BǪRN: *see* BARN

C-: *see* K-

DAGR, m., day: nom. sg. dagr, 24.4; acc. sg. dag, 11.6, 12.3, 23.5, 40.3, 41.3; gen. sg. dags, 25.2

DALR, m., valley: acc. pl. dala, 14.6

DEILA, wk. v., to separate, distinguish, share: 3 pers. sg. pres. deilir, 15.5, 16.2; 1 pers. sg. pret. with enclitic pronoun deildac, 55.8 (note)

DEYIA, str. v., to die: 3 pers. pl. pres. deyia, 43.7, 47.5

DÓTTIR, f., daughter: acc. sg. dóttur, 47.1

DRAGA, str. v., to drag, draw: 3 pers. sg. pres. dregr, 11.5, 12.2, 13.5, 14.2

DRÓTT, f., court, company, people: acc. sg. drótt, 24.5

DRÓTTMEGIR, m. pl., people, host: acc. pl. dróttmǫgo, 11.6, 12.3

DUGA, wk. v., to aid (with dat.), to endure, be strong or sufficient (abs.): 3 pers. pres. sg. dugir, 20.2, 22.2; 3 pers. pres. sg. subj. dugi, 4.4

DǪGG, f., dew: nom. sg. dǫgg, 14.6

EC, 1 pers. sg. prn., I: nom. ec, 1.5, 2.2, 2.5, 3.1, 3.2, 3.3, 3.4, 6.2, 6.4, 8.1, 8.5, 10.5, 35.4, 43.3, 43.4, 43.5, 44.1, 44.2, 44.3, 46.1, 46.2, 46.3, 48.1, 48.2, 48.3, 50.1, 50.2, 50.3, 52.1, 52.2, 52.3, 54.1, 54.3, 55.5, 55.7; acc. mic, 1.2; dat. mér, 1.1, 1.5, 11.1

EF, conj., if, whether, 6.5, 20.2, 22.2

EIGA, pret.-pres. v., to have: 3 pers. sg. pret. átti, 5.5

EIGN, f., possession: dat. pl. eignom, 50.5

EINHERIAR, m. pl., warriors in Valhǫll: nom. einheriar, 41.1 (note)

EINN, adj., one, only: str. f. acc. sg. eina, 47.1; wk. n. acc. sg. 20.1; str. f. nom. pl. einar, 49.4 (note)

EITRDROPI, m., drop of poison: nom. pl. eitrdropar, 31.2

ELLIPTI, ord. number, eleventh: wk. n. acc. sg. ellipta, 40.1

ELLZTR: see GAMALL

EM(C): see VERA

ENDI, m., end, edge: dat. sg. enda, 37.2

ENGI, adj., no, none: str. m. acc. sg. engi, 2.4

EN(N), adv., but, 21.3 (note), 21.6, 25.3, 27.3, 29.6, 45.2

ENN, 32.5: see INN

ER, indecl. rel. prn., who, which, 7.2, 10.2, 10.6, 11.5, 12.2, 13.5, 14.2, 15.5, 16.2, 17.5, 18.2, 24.5, 37.2, 48.5

ER, conj., when, 32.6, 35.5, 44.5, 46.6, 47.5, 50.6, 51.3, 52.6

ER, 7.1, 18.5, 18.6, 23.2, 25.2, 27.2, 31.6: see VERA

ERO, ERT(U): see VERA

ET: see INN

EY, adv., always, 12.6; never, 55.1 (note)

EYRA, n., ear: acc. or dat. sg. eyra, 54.6, 55.3

EÞA, conj., or, and, 6.6, 9.6, 10.3, 20.5, 22.6, 24.6, 26.5, 28.5, 34.5

FALLA, str. v., to fall: 3 pers. pres. pl. falla, 49.2 (note)

FARA, str. v., to go, travel, overtake: inf. fara, 1.2; 3 pers. sg. pres. ferr, 22.5, 24.5, 36.5; 3 pers. pl. pres. fara, 48.6; 2 pers. sg. pres. subj. farir, 4.1; 3 pers. sg. pres. subj. fari, 47.3; 1 pers. sg. pret. fór, 3.1, 44.1, 46.1, 48.1, 50.1, 52.1, 54.1; 3 pers. sg. pret. fór, 5.1; imp. sg. far, 19.2; imp. sg. with enclitic pers. prn. farþu, 9.3; pret. part. str. n. nom. sg. farit, 8.5, 46.6 (note)

FAÞIR, m., father: nom. sg. faþir, 5.5, 23.2, 25.2, 27.2, 29.5

FEIGR, adj., fated to die: str. m. dat. sg. feigom, 55.4

FELLA, wk. v., to let fall: 3 pers. sg. pres. fellir, 14.4

FERR: *see* FARA

FIMTI, ord. number, fifth: wk. n. acc. sg. fimta, 28.1

FINNA, str. v., to find, meet: md. 3 pers. pl. pres. finnaz, 17.5, 18.2

FIÓRÐI, ord. number, fourth: wk. n. acc. sg. fiórða, 26.1

FIRAR, m. pl., human beings, men: dat. pl. firom, 44.6

FIQLÞ, f. (great quantity) as adv., much, 3.1, 3.2, 3.3, 44.1, 44.2, 44.3, 46.1, 46.2, 46.3, 48.1, 48.2, 48.3, 50.1, 50.2, 50.3, 52.1, 52.2, 52.3, 54.1, 54.2, 54.3

FLEIRA: *see* MARGR

FORN, adj., old, ancient: str. m. dat. pl. fornom, 1.5; str. m. acc. pl. forna, 55.5

FORVITNI, f., curiosity: acc. sg. forvitni, 1.4

FÓR: *see* FARA

FÓTR, m., foot, leg: nom. sg. fótr, 33.4; dat. sg. fœti, 33.4

FRAM, adv., early, before: sup. fremst, 34.5

FRAMI, m., fame: gen. sg. frama, 11.3, 13.3, 15.3, 17.3

FRÁ, prep., with dat., from, concerning, 7.5, 41.5, 42.4, 43.1

FREISTA, wk. v. with gen. or abs., to attempt, test, seek: inf. freista, 5.2, 9.4, 11.3, 13.3, 15.3, 17.3; 1 pers. sg. pret. freistaða, 3.2; 1 pers. sg. pret. with enclitic pers. prn. freistaþac, 44.2, 46.2, 48.2, 50.2, 52.2, 54.2

FREMST: *see* FRAM

FRÓDGEDIAÞR, adj., wise: str. f. nom. pl. fródgediaþar, 48.6

FRÓÞR, adj., wise: str. m. nom. sg. fróþr, 6.5, 19.1; wk. m. nom. sg. fróþi, 20.6, 30.6, 35.5; str. m. acc. sg. fróþan, 26.2, 28.2, 34.2; wk. m. gen. sg. fróða, 33.5; str. n. acc. pl. fróþ, 26.6

FYR, FYRIR, prep.: 1) with acc., fyr neðan, beneath, 43.6; 2) abs., as adv., forth, 9.2

FYRR, adv., sooner, earlier: sup. fyrst, 6.4, 20.6, 26.6, 30.6, 34.4, 35.4

FŒTI: *see* FÓTR

GAMALL, adj., old: wk. m. nom. sg. gamli, 9.6; sup. m. nom. sg. ellztr, 28.4

GAMAN, n., joy, pleasure: acc. sg. gaman, 32.6

GANGA, f., a walking, journey: dat. sg. gǫngo, 8.2

GANGA, str. v., to walk, go: 3 pers. sg. pret. gecc, 5.6

GARÐR, m., enclosure, courtyard: dat. pl. gǫrðom, 2.3

GECC: *see* GANGA

GEÐSPEKI, f., intelligence, wisdom: acc. sg. geðspeki, 19.6

GESTR, m., guest, stranger: nom. sg. gestr, 9.6, 19.1, 19.6

GETA, str. v., to acquire, beget: 3 pers. sg. pres. subj. geti, 10.5; 3 pers. sg. pret. gat, 32.4, 33.5

GÍSLING, f., hostage: dat. sg. gíslingo, 39.3

GLEYPA, wk. v., to swallow: inf. gleypa, 53.1

GOD, n., god, divinity: nom. pl. goð, 17.6, 18.3; gen. pl. goða, 2.3, 42.5, 43.2, 50.5, 51.2; dat. pl. goðom, 15.6, 16.3, 39.3

GÓÐR, adj., good: sup. str. m. nom. sg. beztr, 12.4

GÓLF, n., floor: dat. sg. gólfi, 9.2, 11.2, 13.2, 15.2, 17.2

GRUND, f., field, grassy plain: acc. sg. grund, 15.6, 16.3

GÝGR, f., giantess: gen. sg. gýgiar, 32.6

GǪNGO: *see* GANGA

HAFA, wk. v., to have, possess: inf. hafa, 51.5; 1 pers. sg. pres. hefi, 8.5, 43.4; 3 pers. sg. pres. hefir, 46.6; 3 pers. pl. pres. hafa, 45.5; 3 pers. sg. pret. hafdit with negative enclitic, 32.6

HALR, m., man, warrior: nom. pl. halir, 43.7

HAMINGJA, f., guardian spirit: nom. pl. hamingior, 49.4 (note)

HAMR, m., skin, shape: dat. sg. ham, 37.3

HANA: see HON

HANN, m. 3 pers. sg. prn., he: nom. sg. hann, 5.4, 12.5, 14.5, 18.5, 23.2, 25.2, 27.2, 32.6, 38.7, 38.8, 39.5, 53.5; acc. sg. hann, 36.6, 39.2; gen. sg. hans, 37.4

HAUSS, m., skull: dat. sg. hausi, 21.4

HEILL, adj., hale, safe: str. m. nom. sg. heill, 4.1 (note), 4.2, 4.3, 6.1 (as a greeting)

HEIM, adv., homewards, 39.6

HEIMA, adv., at home, 2.1

HEIMR, m., (region of the) world, realm of beings: acc. sg. heim, 43.4; dat. sg. heimi, 49.5; gen. pl. heima, 43.5 (note)

HEITA, str. v., to be called: 1 pers. sg. pres. heiti, 8.1; 3 pers. sg. pres. heitir, 11.4, 12.1, 13.4, 14.1, 15.4, 16.1, 17.4, 18.1, 23.1, 25.1, 27.1, 37.1

HEL, f., hell, death: dat. sg. helio, 4

HENDI: see HǪND

HESTR, m., horse: nom. sg. hestr, 11.4; gen. pl. hesta, 12.4

HIMINN, m., heaven: nom. sg. himinn, 21.4; acc. sg. himin, 23.4, 46.5; gen. sg. himins, 37.2

HINIG, adv., thither, 43.7

HINN, demonstrative prn., that, this (emphatically): n. acc. sg. hitt, 3.4, 6.4

HOF, n., temple, hall: dat, pl. hofom, 38.6 (note)

HOLD, n., flesh: dat. sg. holdi, 21.1

HOLT, n., wood, grove: dat. sg. holti, 45.3

HON, f. 3 pers. sg. prn., she: nom. sg. hon, 16.5; acc. sg. hana, 47.3

HRÍMKALDR, adj., rime-cold, frost-cold: wk. m. gen. sg. hrímkalda, 21.5

HRÍMÞURS, m., frost-giant: dat. sg. hrímþursi, 33.2

HUNDRAÞ, n., hundred: nom. sg. hundraþ, 18.4

HUNNMARGR, adj., hundred-fold: str. n. dat. pl. hunnmǫrgom, 38.7

HVAÐAN, interrog., whence, 20.4, 22.4, 24.4, 26.4, 30.4, 36.4, 38.4, 46.4 (note)

HVAR, interrog., where, 40.2

HVARS (= hvar er), adv., wherever, 4.5

HVAT, interrog., what, 7.1, 34.4, 44.4, 52.4, 54.4, 55.2

HVÁRR, indef. prn., whoever, which of two: m. nom. sg. hvárr, 9.5

HVERFA, str. v., to turn about (in a circle): inf. hverfa, 23.4

HVERN, = HVERIA(N): see HVERR, 2)

HVERR, 1) indef. prn., interrog., who, whoever, what: m. nom. sg. hverr, 28.4; m. dat. sg. hveim, 10.6; m. nom. pl. hverir, 50.4; f. nom. pl. hveriar, 48.4; 2) adj., each: str. m. acc. sg. hverian, 11.5, 14.5, 18.5, 23.5, 40.3, 41.3, 43.4 (hvern); str. f. acc. sg. hveria, 14.2

HVÉ, interrog, adv. how, in what way, 3.5, 11.4, 13.4, 15.4, 17.4, 32.4

HVÍ, interrog, why, 9.1, 42.2 (note)

HYGGIA, wk. v., to think, believe: 1 pers. sg. pres. hygg, 10.5; 1 pers. sg. pret. hugða, 2.5

HǪFUÐ, n., head: dat. sg. hǫfði, 19.4

HǪGGVA, str. v., to cut, strike at: md. 3 pers. pl. pres. hǫggvaz, 40.3, 41.3

HǪLL, f., hall: acc. sg. hǫll, 6.2; dat. sg. hǫllo, 5.4, 19.5; dat. pl. hǫllom, 7.5

HǪND, f., arm: dat. sg. hendi, 33.1

HǪRGR, m., altar, heathen shrine: dat. pl. hǫrgom, 38.6 (note)

IAFNRAMMR, adj., as strong as: str. m. acc. sg. iafnramman, 2.5

ILLA, adv., badly: 10.5

INN, definite article, the: m. nom. sg. inn, 7.6, 9.6, 20.6, 30.6, 32.5 (enn), 35.5, 42.7, 44.5; m. acc. sg. inn, 1.6, 12.2, 46.5; n. acc. sg. iþ, 20.1, 22.6, 23.3, 24.1 26.1, 28.1, 30.1, 32.1, 34.1, 36.1, 38.1, 40.1 (et), 42.1, 42.6; m. gen. sg. ins, 5.3, 21.5, 33.5; n. nom. pl. in, 17.6, 18.3

INN, adv., in, inwards, 5.6

IÓR, m., stallion: nom. sg. iór, 13.4

IÞ: *see* INN

IQRÐ, f., earth: nom. sg. iǫrð, 20.4, 21.2. 29.2 (iǫrþ), 35.2

IǪTUNN, m., giant: nom. sg. iǫtunn, 6.6, 8.6, 20.6, 30.6, 31.3, 32.5, 34.6, 35.5, 37.3, 42.7; acc. sg. iǫtun, 1.6, 2.4, 4.6; gen. sg. iǫtuns, 5.3, 19.2, 21.5, 33.5; gen. pl. iǫtna, 15.5, 16.2, 30.5, 42.4, 43.1; dat. pl. iǫtnom, 49.6

Í, prep.: 1) with acc., into, during, 6.2, 9.3, 28.6, 39.4, 55.2; 2) with dat., in, within, 2.3, 7.2, 9.3, 19.3, 19.5, 37.3, 39.1, 40.2, 41.2, 45.3, 49.5, 54.6, 55.3

ÍSS, m., ice: nom. sg. íss, 16.6

KALDR, adj., cold, hostile: str. m. acc. pl. kalda, 53.4 (note)

KALDRIFIADR, adj., "cold-ribbed," cunning, hostile: str. m. acc. sg. kaldrifiadan, 10.6 (note)

KANN: *see* KUNNA

KIAPTR, m., jaw: acc. pl. kiapta, 53.4

KIÓSA, str. v., to choose: 3 pers. pl. pres. kiósa, 41.4

KLYFIA, wk. v., to cleave, break apart: inf. klyfia, 53.5

KOMA, str. v., to come, arrive: inf. koma, 37.5, 39.5; 3 pers. sg. pres. kømr, 10.2, 10.6, 14.6, 36.4, 46.4 (cømr); 2 pers. sg. pres. subj. komir, 4.2, 7.4 (comir); 1 pers. sg. pret. kom, 43.5 (note); 3 pers. sg. pret. com, 5.4, 20.4, 22.4 (kom), 24.4, 26.4, 30.5, 38.4 (kom); 3 pers. pl. pret. kómu, 31.5; pret. part. str. m. nom. sg. kominn, 6.2, 8.2; pret. part. str. n. nom. sg., komit, 43.4 (note)

KUNNA, pret.-pres. v., to know, be able: 3 pers. sg. pres. kann, 43.3

LAÐAR: *see* LǪD

LEGGIA, wk. v., to lay: pret. part. str. m. nom. sg. lagiðr, 35.6

LENGI, adv., for a long time, 8.5

LETIA, str. v., to dissuade: inf. letia, 2.1 (note)

LEYNA, wk. v., to hide, conceal: md. inf. leynaz, 45.2

LIFA, wk. v., to live: 3 pers. sg. pres. lifir, 44.4

LÍÞA, str. v., to pass, move: 3 pers. sg. pres. líþr, 44.5; 3 pers. pl. pres. líþa, 48.5

LÚÐR, m., cradle: acc. sg. lúðr, 35.6 (note)

LÝSA, wk. v., to shine: 3 pers. sg. pres. lýsir, 12.6

LǪÐ, f., invitation, hospitality: gen sg. laðar, 8.4

MAN(T): *see* MUNA

MARGR, adj., many: comp. n. acc. sg. fleira, 9.5

MARR, m., sea: acc. sg. mar, 48.5

MARR, m., steed: dat. sg. mari, 12.6

MATR, m., food: dat. sg. mat, 45.5

MAÞR, m., human being, man: nom. sg. maþr, 10.1; dat. sg. manne, 55.1 (note); nom. pl. menn, 36.6; acc. pl. menn, 22.5, 37.6; gen. pl. manna, 7.1, 44.4

MÁNI, m., moon: nom. sg. máni, 22.4; gen. sg. mána, 23.2

MEIRR: *see* MIǪK

MEY, MEYIA(R): *see* MÆR

MEÞ, prep.: 1) with dat., with, among, between, 12.5, 15.5, 15.6, 16.2, 16.3, 24.6, 30.5, 38.5, 39.6, 44.6, 49.6; 2) with acc., towards, 26.6

MÉLDROPI, m., drop of foam from a horse's bit: acc. pl. méldropa, 14.4

MÉR: *see* EC

MIC: *see* EC

MICILL, adj., great: str. f. nom. sg. micil, 10.4; str. f. acc. sg. micla, 1.4

MINN, possessive adj., my, mine: f. acc. sg. mína, 55.8; m. dat. sg. mínom, 7.2; m. acc. pl. mína, 55.5

MIǪK, adv., much: comp. meirr, 41.6

MORGINDǪGG, f., morning dew: acc. pl. morgindǫggvar, 45.4 (note)

MORGINN, m., morning: acc. sg. morgin, 14.5

MÓDIR, f., mother: gen. sg. módur, 47.6

MUNA, pret.-pres. verb, to remember: 1 pers. sg. pres. man, 35.4; 2 pers. sg. pres. mant, 34.4

MUNNR, m., mouth: dat. sg. munni, 55.4

MUNU, pret.-pres. v., will (as aux.): 3 pers. sg. pres. mun, 39.5, 53.2, 53.3, 53.5; 3 pers. pl. pres. muno, 45.2; 1 pers. sg. pret. subj. munda, 2.2 (note)

MÆLA, wk. v., to speak (abs.), address (with acc.): inf. mæla, 4.6; md. 1 pers. pl. pres. mælomc, 19.3; md. 2 pers. sg. pres. mæliz, 9.2; 3 pers. sg. pres. subj. mæli, 10.3; 1 pers. sg. pret. mælta, 55.5; 3 pers. sg. pret. mælti, 54.4

MÆR, f., maiden, girl: nom. sg. mær, 47.6; acc. sg. mey, 33.3; nom. pl. meyiar, 48.4; gen. pl. meyia, 49.3

MÆRR, adj., famous, glorious: wk. m. nom. sg. mæra, 44.5

MǪGR, m., youth, son: acc. sg. mǫg, 33.3

MǪN, f., mane: nom. sg. mǫn, 12.6

NEDAN, adv., from below, 43.6 (see FYR)

NEMA, conj., unless, 7.6

NÉ, neg. particle, not, 7.4

NIÐ, f., waning moon: acc. sg. niþ, 25.4; dat. pl. niðom, 24.6

NIÐR, m., son, kinsman: gen. pl. niðia, 28.5

NÍO, indecl. card. number, nine, 43.5

NÍUNDI, ord. number, ninth: wk. n. acc. sg. niunda, 36.1

NÓTT, f., night: nom. sg. nótt, 24.6, 25.3; acc. sg. nótt, 13.6, 14.3

NÚ, adv., now, 1.1, 6.1, 6.2, 8.2, 19.1, 55.7

NÝ, n., waxing moon: acc. sg. ný, 25.4

NÝTR, adj., able, capable: str. n. nom. pl. nýt, 25.5; str. n. acc. pl. nýt, 13.6, 14.3

OC, conj., and, 5.5 (note), 8.6, 15.6, 16.3, 17.6, 18.3, 19.3, 20.3, 22.3, 23.3, 24.3, 25.4, 26.3, 28.3, 30.3, 32.3, 33.3, 34.3, 36.3, 38.6, 38.8, 39.3, 41.5, 42.5, 43.2, 45.1, 51.1, 51.4, 51.6, 55.6

OF, prep., with acc., over, throughout, 11.6, 13.6, 14.3

OFRMÆLGI, f., vaunting, boasting, garrulity: nom. sg. ofrmælgi, 10.4

OPINN, adj., open, unfrozen: str. f. nom. sg. opin, 16.4

ORÐ, n., word, speech: dat. sg. orði, 7.3; dat. pl. orðom, 4.6

ORÞSPECI, f., cleverness or wisdom in words: acc. sg. orþspeci, 55.8; gen. sg. orþspeci, 5.2

ÓAUÞIGR, adj., unwealthy, poor: str. m. nom. sg. óauþigr, 10.1

OR, prep., with dat., out of, from: 21.1, 21.3, 21.4, 21.6, 31.1, 31.3, 43.7

ÓRAR, ÓROM: *see* VÁRR

ÓX: *see* VAXA

QVEÞA, str. v., to speak, say, declare: 1 pers. sg. pres. qveþ, 1.5; 3 pers. pl. pres. qveþa, 24.2, 26.2, 28.2, 30.2, 32.2, 34.2, 36.2, 37.5; 3 pers. sg. pret. qvaþ, 18, 19, 20, 21, 22, 23, 24, 25, 26, 27, 28, 29, 30, 31, 32, 33, 34, 35, 36, 37, 38, 39, 40, 41, 42, 43, 44, 45, 46, 47, 48, 49, 50, 51, 52, 53, 54, 55; 3 pers. pl. pret qváþo, 33.2

RASTA: *see* RǪST

RÁÐA, str. v. with dat. or abs., to advise, counsel, rule: 3 pers. sg. pres. ræðr, 38.7; 3 pers. pl. ráþa, 50.4; pres. imp. ráþ, 1.1

RECA, str. v. with gen., to avenge: inf. reca, 53.3 (note)

REGIN, n. pl., the gods, divine powers: nom. regin, 25.5, 39.2, 47.5, 52.6; acc. regin, 3.3, 13.6, 14.3, 26.6, 44.3, 46.3, 48.3, 50.3, 52.3, 54.3; gen. ragna, 55.6

RENNA, str. v., to run, flow: inf. renna, 16.4

REYNA, wk. v., to test, examine, explore: 1 pers. sg. pret. reynda, 3.3, 44.3, 46.3, 48.3, 50.3, 52.3, 54.3

RIÚFA, str. v., to break, be destroyed: md. 3 pers. pl. pres. riúfaz, 52.6

RÍÐA, str. v., to ride: inf. ríða, 47.4; 3 pers. pl. pres. ríþa, 41.5

RO: *see* VERA

RÚN, f., secret, mystery: dat. pl. rúnom, 42.4, 43.1

RÆÐR: *see* RÁDA

RǪC, n. pl., fates, judgments, (hence in regard to eschatology) destruction: acc. rǫc, 38.2, 39.4, 42.2, 55.6

RǪST, f., the distance between two resting places in a journey: gen. pl. rasta, 18.4 (note)

SALAKYNNI, n. pl., home, homestead: nom. salakynni, 3.6

SALR, m., hall: dat. sg. sal, 7.2, 9.3; gen. pl. sala, 8.3

SAMAN, adv., together, 19.3, 31.5, 33.3, 41.6

SAMR, adj., same: wk. n. acc. sg. sama, 22.6, 23.3

SANNR, adj., true: str. n. acc. sg. satt, 43.3; sup. wk. n. acc. sg. sannasta, 42.6

SATT: *see* SANNR

SÁ, m. demonstrative prn., he, the: nom. sg. sá, 11.4, 13.4, 17.4, 18.6, 24.5, 32.4, 35.5; acc. sg. þann, 1.6; gen. sg. þess, 5.3, 29.5; nom. pl. þeir, 41.4; dat. pl. þeim, 18.6

SÁTTR, adj., reconciled, at peace: str. m. nom. pl. sáttir, 41.6

SCAL(T): *see* SCULU

SCAPA, str. and wk. v., to make, create: 3 pers. pret. pl. scópo, 25.5, 39.2; pret. part. str. f. nom. sg. scǫpuð, 21.2, 29.2, 35.2

SCÍRR, adj., bright, shining: wk. m. acc. sg. scíra, 12.2

SCULU, pret.-pres. v., must, ought (as aux.): 2 pers. sg. pres. scalt, 4.5; 3 pers. sg. pres. scal, 9.4, 16.5, 47.4; 1 pers. pl. pres. scolom, 19.5; 3 pers. pl. pres. scolo, 23.5, 51.5

SEGIA, wk. v., to say, relate: inf. segia, 43.3; 2 pers. sg. pres. segir, 42.6; 2 pers. sg. pret. subj. sagdir, 55.3; imp. sg. with enclitic prn. segþu, segðu, segdu, 11.1, 13.1, 15.1, 17.1, 20.1, 22.1, 24.1, 26.1, 28.1, 30.1, 32.1, 34.1, 36.1, 38.1, 40.1, 42.1

SELIA, wk. v., to give: 3 pers. pl. pret. seldo, 39.3

SEM, conj., as, 2.6

SESS, m., seat: acc. sg. sess, 9.3; dat. sg. sessi, 19.3

SEXHǪFÐAÞR, adj., six-headed: str. m. acc. sg. sexhǫfðaþan, 33.6

SÉ: *see* VERA

SÉR, 4.3, 6.5, 7.6, *see* VERA; 45.5, *see* SIK

SÉTTI, ord. number, sixth: wk. n. acc. sg. sétta, 30.1

SIAUNDI, ord. number, seventh: wk. n. acc. sg. siaunda, 32.1

SIÁ, demonstrative prn., this: f. acc. sg. þessa, 46.6

SIÁ, str. v., to see: inf. siá 6.3; 3 pers. pl. pres. siá, 36.6

SIÁLFR, adj., him-, her-, itself: str. m. nom. sg. siálfr, 54.6; str. m. acc. sg. siálfan, 6.3, 36.6

SIK, refl. prn., him-, her-, itself: dat. pl. sér, 45.5

SINNI, n., fellowship, company: dat. pl. sinnom, 4.3 (note)

SIÓR, m., sea: nom. sg. siór, 21.6

SITIA, str. v., to sit: 3 pers. sg. pres. sitr, 37.2; 3 pers. pl. pres. sitia, 41.6

SLÉTTR, adj., smooth, level: wk. m. acc. sg. slétta, 46.5

SLOCNA, wk. v., to be extinguished: 3 pers. sg. pres. slocnar, 50.6, 51.3

SNOTR, adj., wise: comp. m. nom. sg. snotrari, 7.6

SONR, m., son: acc. sg. son, 33.6; dat. sg. syni, 54.6, 55.3; dat. pl. sonom, 15.5, 16.2, 30.5, 38.5

SÓL, f., sun: nom. sg. sól, 22.6, 46.4; gen. sg. sólar, 23.3

STAFR, m., stave, letter, (hence) wisdom: acc. pl. stafi, 55.5; dat. pl. stǫfom, 1.5

STÍGA, str. v., to walk, ascend: 3 pers. sg. pret. subj. stigi, 54.5

STØCCVA, str. v., to spring forth, be sprinkled: 3 pers. pl. pret. stucco, 31.2

SUMAR, n., summer: nom. sg. sumar, 26.5; gen. sg. sumars, 27.3

SÚ, f. demonstrative prn., she, the: nom. sg. sú, 15.4, 47.4; nom. pl. þær, 48.4, 49.6.

SVÁ, adv., so, thus, 22.5, 23.3, 31.3, 36.5

SVÁSS, adj., dear, beloved: wk. n. nom. pl. sváso, 17.6, 18.3

SVEITI, m., sweat, blood: dat. sg. sveita, 21.6 (note)

SVINNR, adj., wise: str. m. acc. sg. svinnan, 24.2, 30.2, 32.2, 36.2

SYNI: see SONR

TIL, 1) prep., with gen., to, 8.3, 10.2; 2) adv., too, 31.6

TÍDA, wk. v. impers., to long for, wish: 3 pers. sg. pres. tíðir, 1.2

TÍUNDI, ord. number, tenth: wk. n. acc. sg. tíunda, 38.1

TÍVAR, m., gods: gen pl. tíva, 38.2, 42.2

TÓLFTI, ord. number, twelfth: wk. n. acc. sg. tólfta, 42.1

TÚN, n., home meadow, enclosure: dat. pl. túnom, 40.2, 41.2

UM, 1) prep., with acc., over, throughout, about: 12.3, 14.6, 16.5, 19.6, 55.6; 2) untranslatable preverbal particle, 11.3 (note), 13.3, 15.3, 17.3, 20.4, 21.2, 22.4, 24.4, 26.4, 34.5, 35.2, 35.4, 35.6, 36.4, 36.6, 38.4, 41.6, 43.4

UNDIR, prep., with dat., under, beneath, 33.1

UNZ, conj., until, 31.3

UPHIMINN, m., heaven above: nom. sg. uphiminn, 20.5

ÚLFR, m., wolf: nom. sg. úlfr, 53.1

ÚT, adv., out, 7.4

VALR, m., those slain in battle: acc. sg. val, 41.4

VANR, m., god: dat. pl. vǫnom, 39.6

VAR: *see* VERA

VARÐ: *see* VERÐA

VARMR, adj., warm: str. n. nom. sg., varmt, 26.5

VARR, possessive prn., our, ours: f. nom. pl. órar, 31.4; f. dat. pl. órom, 7.5

VARÞAÞ: *see* VERÐA

VAXA, str. v., to grow: inf. vaxa, 33.1; 3 pers. sg. pret. óx, 31.3

VÁGR, m., wave, sea: acc. sg. vág, 36.5

VEÐIA, wk. v., to wager (with dat.): inf. veðia, 19.4

VEGR, m., way, direction: acc. sg. veg, 18.5

VEIT, VETZT: *see* VITA

VERA, irregular v., to be: inf. vera, 2.6; 1 pers. sg. pres. em, 6.2; 1 pers. sg. pres. with enclitic pers. prn. emc, 8.2; 2 pers. sg. pres. ert, 34.6, 55.9; 2 pers. sg. pres. with enclitic pers. prn. ertu, 19.1; 3 pers. sg. pres. er, 7.1, 18.5, 18.6, 23.2, 25.2, 27.2, 31.6; 3 pers. pl. pres. ro, ero, 48.4, 49.5; 2 pers. sg. pres. subj. sér, 4.3, 6.5, 7.6; 3 pers. pl. pres. subj. sé, 3.6; 3 pers. sg. pret. var, 21.2, 25.3, 29.3, 29.5, 35.3, 35.6; 3 pers. sg. pret. subj. væri, 29.2, 35.2

VERÐA, str. v., to happen, become (of): 3 pers. sg. pres. verþr, 52.4; 3 pers. sg. pres. with negative enclitic verþrat, 16.6; 3 pers. sg. pret. varð, 31.3; 3 pers. sg. pret. with negative enclitic varþaþ, 38.8 (as aux.); 3 pers. sg. pret. subj. yrþi, 28.6

VERPA, str. v. with dat., to throw, cast: md. 1 pers. sg. pres. verpomc, 7.3 (note)

VERR, m., male, male being: gen. pl. vera, 55.9

VETR, m., winter, year: nom. sg. vetr, 26.4; gen. sg. vetrar, 27.2; gen. pl. vetra, 29.1, 35.1

VÉ, n., abode, temple: acc. sg. vé, 51.2 (note)

VIÐ, VIÞ, prep.: 1) with acc., towards, 1.6, 10.6, 55.7; 2) with dat., against, near, on, 33.4

VIÐ, 2 pers. sg. dual pers. prn., we two; nom. við, 19.5

VILJA, irregular v., to wish: 1 pers. sg. pres. vil, 3.4, 6.4; 2 pers. sg. pres. vill, 11.2, 13.2, 15.2, 17.2

VINDR, m., wind: nom. sg. vindr, 36.4; acc. sg. vind, 37.5

VINNA, str. v., to perform, work: inf. vinna, 51.6

VITA, pret.-pres. v., to know: inf. vita, 3.4, 6.4; 2 pers. sg. pres. veitzt, 34.5; 3 pers. sg. pres. veit, 55.1; 2 pers. sg. pres. subj. vitir, 20.3, 22.3, 24.3, 26.3, 28.3, 30.3, 32.3, 34.3, 36.3, 38.3, 42.3; 3 pers. sg. pres. subj. viti, 9.5; pret. part. str. m. nom. sg. vitaþr, 18.6

VITIA, wk. v. with gen., to call on, visit: inf. vitia, 1.3

VITNIR, m., wolf: gen. sg. vitnis, 53.6

VÍG, n., battle: dat. sg. vígi, 17.5, 18.2, 41.5, 53.6

VÍGÞROT, n., end of the battle: dat. sg. vígþroti, 51.6

VÍSS, adj., wise: sup. str. m. nom. sg. vísastr, 55.9; str. n. nom. pl. vís, 39.2; str. m. dat. pl. vísom, 39.6

VÆNGR, m., wing: dat. pl. vængiom, 37.4

VÆRI: see VERA

VǪLLR, m., plain: nom. sg. vǫllr, 17.4, 18.1, 18.6

VǪNOM: see VANR

YFIR, prep., with acc., over, above, 22.5, 24.5, 36.5, 37.6, 48.5, 49.2

YRÞI: see VERDA

ÝTAR, m. pl., mariners, men: nom. ýtar, 40.2

ÞADAN, adv., thence, 14.6, 45.6

ÞANN: see SÁ

ÞAR, adv., there, 31.4

ÞARFR, adj., useful, needful: wk. n. acc. sg. used substantivally, 10.3

ÞAT, n., demonstrative prn., it, that, the: nom. sg. þat, 7.1, 31.6; acc. sg. þat, 13.1, 15.1, 17.1, 20.1, 22.1, 24.1, 26.1, 28.1, 30.1, 32.1, 34.1, 35.4, 36.1, 38.1, 40.1, 42.1, 55.1; gen. sg. þess, 53.3; dat. sg. því, 31.6 (therefore [note]); nom. pl. þau, ðau, 23.5, 45.2, 45.5; gen. pl. þeira, 49.5

ÞÁ, adv., then, 5.1, 9.1, 9.4, 29.3, 35.3, 44.5, 46.6, 47.5, 50.6, 51.3, 52.6

ÞEGAR, adv., immediately, quickly, 5.6

ÞEGIA, wk. v., to be silent: 3 pers. sg. pres. subj. þegi, 10.3

ÞEIM: see SÁ

ÞEIR: see SÁ

ÞEIRA: see ÞAT

ÞESS: see SÁ and ÞAT

ÞESSA: see SIÁ

ÞÉR: see ÞÚ

ÞIC: see ÞÚ

ÞINN, possessive prn., your, yours: n. nom. sg. þitt, 20.2, 22.2; m. gen. sg. þíns, 11.3, 13.3, 15.3, 17.3; m. gen. pl. þinna, 8.3; n. gen. pl. þinna, 8.6

ÞIÓÐ, f., people, nation, race: gen. sg. þióðar, 49.1 (note)

ÞITT: see ÞINN

ÞORP, n., village: acc. pl. þorp, 49.2

ÞÓ, conj., although, 49.6

ÞRIÐI, ord. number, third: wk. n. acc. sg. þriðia, 24.1

ÞRÍR, card. number, three: f. nom. pl. þriár, 49.1

ÞULR, m., wise man, spokesman: nom. sg. þulr, 9.6 (note)

ÞURFI, wk. adj., in need of, lacking: m. nom. sg. þurfi, 8.4

ÞÚ, 2 pers. sg. prn., thou: nom. þú, 1.1, 4.1, 4.2, 4.3, 4.5, 6.1, 6.5, 7.4, 7.6, 9.1, 11,2, 13.2, 15.2, 17.2, 19.2, 20.3, 22.3, 24.3 26.3, 28.3, 30.3, 32.3, 34.3, 34.4, 34.6, 36.3, 38.2, 42.2, 42.6, 55.2, 55.9; acc. þic, þik, 6.3, 24.2, 26.2, 28.2, 30.2, 32.2, 34.2, 36.2; dat. þér, 4.4

ÞVÍ: see ÞAT

ÞVÍAT, conj., since, because (því + at), 2.4, 43.4

ÞYCCIA, wk. v., to seem, appear: 3 pers. sg. pres. þyccir, 12.5

ÞYRSTR, adj., thirsty: str. m. nom. sg. þyrstr, 8.3

ÞÆR: *see* SÚ

Æ, adv., always, 31.6, 55.9, never, 36.6
ÆSIR: *see* ÁSS
ÆTT, f., lineage: nom. pl. ættir, 31.4

ŒÞI, n., mind, disposition: nom. sg. œþi, 4.4, 20.2, 22.2

ØRÓF, n., a great number: dat. sg. ørófi, 29.1 (note), 35.1

QLD, f., age, time, generation: gen. sg. aldar, 39.4; nom. pl. aldir, 45.6; dat.
    pl. qldom, 23.6, 25.6
QLL: *see* ALLR
QRN, m., eagle: gen. sg. arnar, 37.3

INDEX OF NAMES

ÍFING, f., "the violent one," a river: nom. Ífing, 16.1 (note)
ÍMR, m., "the dark looking one," a giant: gen. sg. Íms, 5.5 (note)

LÍF, n., "life," female survivor of the Fimbulvetr: nom. Líf, 45.1
LÍFÐRASIR, m., "persistent life," "abounding in life," survivor of the Fimbulvetr: nom. Lífðrasir, 45.1 (note)

MAGNI, m., son of Þórr: nom. Magni, 51.4 (note)
MIǪLLNIR, m., Þórr's hammer: acc. Miǫllni, 51.6
MÓÞI, m., son of Þórr: nom. Móþi, 51.4
MUNDILFŒRI, m., "the one who carries time," father of the son and moon: nom. Mundilfœri, 23.1 (note)
MǪGÞRASIR, m., "boasting son," "persistent son": gen. Mǫgþrasis, 49.3 (note)

NIFLHEL, f., "dark hell," the region of the dead: acc. Niflhel, 43.6 (note)
NIǪRÐR, m., a god of prosperity, father of Freyr and Freyja: nom. Niǫrðr, 38.4
NǪRR, m., "the narrow one," father of night: dat. Nǫrvi, 25.3 (note)

ÓÐINN, m., the chief god: nom. Óðinn, 5.1, 18, 20, 22, 24, 26, 28, 30, 32, 34, 36, 38, 40, 42, 44, 46, 48, 50, 52, 54, 54.4; acc. Óðin, 55.7; gen. Óðins, 41.2; dat. sg. Óðni, 52.4

REIÐGOTAR, m. pl., "glory-goths," a people: dat. Reiðgotom, 12.5 (note)

SCINFAXI, m., "shining-mane," a horse: nom. Scinfaxi, 12.1
SURTALOGI, m., "the flame of Surtr": nom. Surtalogi, 50.6 (note), 51.3
SURTR, m., a giant who will fight against the gods in the Ragnarǫk: nom. Surtr, 17.6, 18.3

SVÁSUÞR, m., "the mild South (?)," father of summer: nom. Svásuþr, 27.3 (note)

VAFÞRÚÐNIR, m., "the one powerful in tricks," a giant: nom. Vaf-þrúðnir, 6.1, 19, 20.3, 21, 22.3, 23, 24.3, 25, 26.3, 27, 28.3, 29, 30.3, 31, 32.3, 33, 34.3, 35, 36.3, 37, 38.3, 39, 41, 42.3, 43, 45, 47, 49, 51, 53, 55; gen. Vafðrúdnis, Vafðrúþnis, 1.3 (see Introduction p. 35), 3.5; dat. Vafðrúðni, 2.6

VANAHEIMR, m., region of the Vanir: dat. sg. Vanaheimi, 39.1

VÁLI, m., son of Óðinn: nom. Váli, 51.1 (note)

VINDSVALR, adj. as m., "wind-cool," father of winter: nom. Vindsvalr, 27.1 (note)

VÍGRÍÞR, m., "battle-field," a plain: nom. Vígriþr, 18.1 (note)

VÍÞARR, m., son of Óðinn: nom. Víþarr, 51.1, 53.3

YGGR, m., "the terrible one," Óðinn: nom. Yggr, 5.6

YMIR, m., giant from whom the world was created: gen. Ymis, 21.1 (note), 28.5 (note)

ÞRÚDGELMIR, m., "powerful-screamer," a giant, father of Bergelmir: nom. Þrúdgelmir, 29.4